Praise for
Do You Talk Funny?

"David Nihill talks funny. He also writes funny. But his book isn't just entertaining, it's incredibly useful. It's packed with effective and easy-to-implement tips that have helped me in my presentations."

—AJ Jacobs, author of *Drop Dead Healthy* and
The Year of Living Biblically

"Your next talk will be 10 times more entertaining if you read this book."

—Charlie Hoehn, author of *Play It Away:
A Workaholic's Cure for Anxiety*

"This is a book you don't just read, it's a book you DO. Look, I'm such an expert in this field that I'm quoted in the book, and even I learned a tremendous amount reading it, so I'm gonna guess you will, too."

—Bill Grundfest, Golden Globe Winner, three-time
Emmy nominee, and founder of NYC's Comedy Cellar

"It is one of those rare books that makes you think, laugh, and embrace your quirky self. In an inspiring and entertaining manner, *Do You Talk Funny?* teaches you how to find your inner storytelling mojo. A great read!"

—Michael Margolis, author, *Believe Me* and CEO of Get Storied

"I've given quite a few talks and this is the most helpful book I've found on becoming a better speaker. Plus, the book is really funny—I laughed out loud at least five times."

—Justin Mares, coauthor of *Traction: How Any Startup
Can Achieve Explosive Customer Growth*

"This book is practical, actionable, and most importantly, effective. Not only does David nail how to add funny to your talks, he also practices what he preaches in this very entertaining read. My two complaints are: 1) This book didn't exist when I started as a speaker and 2) I didn't write it."

—Andrew Tarvin, author of *Humor That Works*,
award-winning speaker, and NYC-based comedian

"From writing to performing to where to put your hands, David Nihill will help you become a more humorous storyteller. I have been lucky enough to have a beer with the guy—and can confirm that he really does talk funny."

—Peter McGraw, University of Colorado professor, director of the Humor Research Lab (HuRL), coauthor of *The Humor Code: A Global Search for What Makes Things Funny*

"This is a cracker of a book; I really enjoyed it. As a nervous public speaker I know if I can make the audience laugh, it makes everyone (especially me) feel a lot less awkward. In the past I've lucked into a few laughs, but already after reading this book, I'm making changes to my upcoming presentations that I know are going to get some laughs. It's weird listening to comedy now. I can break down why each joke is funny. It's a real eye-opener!"

—Dan Norris, author of *The 7 Day Startup* and *Content Machine*, cofounder of WPCurve.com

"Anyone who wants to influence and connect with audiences more effectively should scoop up *Do You Talk Funny?* immediately. David Nihill combines personal experience, expert research, and practical tips to create—regardless of his protestations to the contrary—a truly magical handbook for presenters."

—Kat Koppett, author of *Training to Imagine*, TEDx speaker, and founder of Koppett + Company

"Read this book and you'll enjoy presenting to people, they'll enjoy listening to you, and crucially they'll happily retain your message. A riveting read, a super story, and awesome advice."

—Neal O'Gorman, CEO of Artomatix

"As someone who runs sales conferences, I know firsthand of the value humor brings to a presentation. I consider this book my blueprint and will do my best to make sure all of our speakers read it before getting on stage at our events."

—Max Altschuler, author of *Hacking Sales* and CEO of Sales Hacker, Inc.

"David has written the owner's manual for adding a much-needed comedic edge to any presentation or speaking gig. It's a perfect balance of how to be funny ha-ha and funny like a clown without being shot in the foot. Some people are born funny; they are called comedians. The rest of us will have to try a bit harder and read this book."

—Jason Miller, author of *Welcome to the Funnel*, keynote speaker, and senior content marketing manager at LinkedIn

"As someone who's given many corporate presentations over the last 15 years, I wish I'd read this book sooner. David generously illustrates a simple formula for creating a connection with an audience using storytelling and honesty. And he does it all with his own brand of wit and humor. A compassionate teacher who practices what he preaches! If you don't know where to start, start with *Do You Talk Funny?* You'll build the tools to become a speaker who's confident, memorable and, most importantly, funny."

—Sarah Cooper, former Google design lead and creator of thecooperreview.com

"As a motivational speaker by circumstance, I have often found myself in situations where somehow the fear of a speaking engagement outweighed the stress of competition. (Truth be told, I wasn't enjoying the challenge!) David Nihill's book does a phenomenal job addressing that fear with some useful tools that I find myself even practicing in daily conversation. I highly recommend this book to those with a fear of public speaking and an interest in approaching it from a different angle. It's a smart book that's engaging, and it works!"

—Cristina Teuscher, Olympic gold and bronze medalist, former U.S. Olympic swim team captain

"In the ever-expanding TED-centric world of public speaking, this book should be compulsory reading for anyone aspiring to be a unique, memorable, and highly entertaining presenter."

—David Howley, Partner at Hedgeserv Ltd.

"David has compiled a great resource for humor lovers and has interwoven lessons he learned from his own experience with what he gleaned from mentors. Glad your father showed you how to squeeze humor out of any situation; now you are helping others do the same!"

—Darren LaCroix, world champion speaker

"I'm a recovering boring person—thanks to the amazing, hilarious, magical, David Nihill. As a speaker, trainer, and human behavior hacker, I use his tips whether I am on stage or in casual conversation. He breaks down humor—a seemingly insurmountable and intimidating topic into easy to understand, practical tips. Stop being boring: Buy this Book!"

–Vanessa Van Edwards, behavioral investigator,
scienceofpeople.com

"We all have short attention spans these days. Increasingly to get noticed you need to be funny. The good news is you can learn how. The even better news is that David can guide you on this journey in an engaging, entertaining, and insightful way. So sit back, relax, and soon you'll be talking funny, too!"

–Philip Madden, founding director of Kennoway Investments

"*DYTF* is a witty and clever take on how to apply the lessons of a business-savvy experimental stand-up comic into today's world of droll and monotonous business presentations. David gives great, practical advice on how to structure any business talk to be as engaging as a five-minute set at the Comedy Cellar. Highly recommended for anyone that has to do corporate presentations for 2- to 5,000-plus-person audiences (and keep them awake and cheering you on)."

–Rob Kniaz, founding partner of Hoxton Ventures

"David's rich life experiences shine through in this wildly entertaining guide to public speaking. Whether you're reading it for fun or to stand out at your next business presentation, I promise you'll be inspired."

–Sami Aziz, producer on ABC's *Shark Tank*,
two-time Emmy award winner

"This book is great. I haven't read it yet but David drew a picture when he was six years old of a penguin drinking beer in a Chinese restaurant and it was clear the potential for slight wisdom and misguided creativity were there."

–Marita Nihill, David's mother

Do You Talk Funny?

Do You Talk funny?

7 Comedy Habits to Become a Better (and Funnier) Public Speaker

DAVID NIHILL

BenBella Books, Inc.
Dallas, Texas

BenBella Books, Inc.
10300 N. Central Expressway
Suite #530
Dallas, TX 75231
www.benbellabooks.com
Send feedback to feedback@benbellabooks.com

Printed in the United States of America

Library of Congress Cataloging-in-Publication Data
Names: Nihill, David, author.
Title: Do you talk funny? : 7 comedy habits to become a better (and funnier) public speaker / David Nihill.
Description: Dallas, TX : BenBella Books, 2016. | Includes bibliographical references and index.
Identifiers: LCCN 2015037723| ISBN 9781942952275 (paperback) | ISBN 9781942952282 (electronic)
Subjects: LCSH: Business presentations. | Wit and humor in business. | BISAC: BUSINESS & ECONOMICS / Business Communication / Meetings & Presentations.
| HUMOR / Topic / Business & Professional. | PERFORMING ARTS / Comedy.
Classification: LCC HF5718.22 .N54 2016 | DDC 658.4/52—dc23 LC record available at http://lccn.loc.gov/2015037723

Copyediting by James Fraleigh
Proofreading by Brittney Martinez and
    Greg Teague
Text design and composition by Aaron
    Edmiston

Front cover by Erin Tyler
Full cover by Sarah Dombrowsky
Printed by Lake Book Manufacturing

Distributed by Perseus Distribution
www.perseusdistribution.com

To place orders through Perseus Distribution:
Tel: (800) 343-4499
Fax: (800) 351-5073
E-mail: orderentry@perseusbooks.com

To my father, Patrick Nihill, who taught me that you can squeeze humor into just about any situation.

Contents

Author's Note

I truly believe we are all funny . . . at least some of the time. Some of us are termed naturally funny and others have to work at it. We all have moments in life that make us laugh. How we communicate those moments to others, in a way most conducive to sharing our joy, is often the missing link. The good news is that this is a skill, which means it can be learned, and few are better placed to help us develop it than comedians.

Comedians' content and delivery are honed through years of practice as they master their craft. In doing so, they are among the few public speakers that clock up the ten thousand hours Malcolm Gladwell says make a master. Yet few of these masters are asked to share their knowledge with a business community who needs it. Almost every book ever written on public speaking says humor is a key part of successful talks. Yet none of them explain well how to employ it, which is about as useful as handing a MacBook Pro to a goat. None of them describe the techniques comedians use in a way beneficial to a business audience. I wanted to address that, so I wrote this book.

Everything in this book I learned the hard way, from people much wiser and more experienced than I. It contains a ton of things that I wish I had known at the start of my journey. They worked for me, and I think they will work for you, too.

Author's Note

If you feel this book doesn't help you become a better and funnier speaker, I am happy to give you a full refund. To claim it, please send a link to a video of your not-so-great speaking performance, along with your receipt, to help@funnybizz.co.

Ten percent of my proceeds for this book will go to Arash Bayatmakou via Help Hope Live until he is fully back on his feet. Thereafter, the 10 percent will go to one of the many facing the same challenges after suffering a severe spinal cord injury.

Introduction

My heartbeat races many beats above normal as I stand, feet firmly planted, on the Castro Theatre's dark hardwood stage, whose construction has stood the test of time. The theater, a historic San Francisco landmark with a Spanish Colonial Baroque façade, has all the grandeur and style that one would expect to accompany its ninety-three years' worth of celebrity performers—one of whom I am very much not. If you had the distinct misfortune to shake my hand before I took the stage, you would have felt like you had been assaulted by a semi-defrosted mackerel.

Despite my distinct lack of fame, eight hundred unfamiliar faces are looking back at me from the assembled crowd. When I arch my neck slightly to look toward the large, stretching ceiling, I am met with the curious gazes of another six hundred faces in the lavish upper-tier balcony. All eyes are firmly on me. On either side of the stage stand large organ grills. Even though I have the musical ability of a dead pigeon, the idea of playing a few notes at this point seems distinctly more appealing than allowing my vocal cords to do what science intended—simply emit words.

To those fourteen hundred pairs of inquisitive eyes in the audience, I probably look calm, collected, and confident.

This is far from the truth. Turbulence is sweeping through my insides. I am so nervous I could lay an egg. I am, however, not just expecting to talk without imploding, a challenge enough in itself for someone with a distinct fear of public speaking—I am going to try and be funny. Moreover, I expect to be so funny that I believe I will not only make these strangers laugh but keep them fully engaged for the next several minutes.

The really crazy part is that not long ago I had never told a joke on stage. I had never even really been on a stage. The truth is that public speaking was, and still is, my single biggest fear. Even more than a stare down with a shark.

Byron Bay, Australia. I took a deep breath and swam within a few feet of the resting shark. He sat oblivious to my attention twenty-five feet below the surface, next to the *Wollongbar*, a sunken ship that lost its tie to the old Byron Bay Pier during a cyclone in 1921 and sank. Long abandoned by its intended occupants, the wreck is now home to Wobbegong sharks, which can grow to ten feet in length. They are the pit bull terriers of the ocean. Their often sleepy demeanor makes them appear passive, but they can leave a serious, lengthy, and rather painful impression.

In February 2004, a snorkeler named Luke Tresoglavic learned this the hard way. Bitten on the leg, Luke swam a thousand feet to shore, walked to his car, and drove to the local surf club . . . with the shark still attached. Luckily for Luke, the shark was young and just two feet long, and he only suffered puncture wounds to his leg from the shark's razor-sharp teeth.

The target of my attention was a bigger creature—an impressive seven feet. I carefully detached my snorkel pipe from my mask and used it to reach out and tap the shark gently to initiate some movement. It obliged, rising and thrusting into motion with the same labored enthusiasm I do whenever I have a 4:00 A.M. flight to catch. As sunlight reflected through the clear waters, I looked upward toward my friends, only to glimpse a sea of bubbles and panicked limbs as they fled the scene of what I am sure they thought was about to be my untimely death.

Most people are afraid of sharks, it seems. I love them. Always have. The story has always rung true in my life: what most people are afraid of, I have been drawn toward. Danger, risk, and fun have always been intertwined for me. Skydiving, cliff jumping, bungee jumping, free diving, poking wild animals—these are exhilarating to me, not terrifying. I don't chase the things that do scare me because being scared is about as pleasant as a cliff jump gone wrong. (Incidentally, when my cliff jumping did once go wrong, it led to a shattered leg on an isolated island, where the only form of medical assistance was a vet. I am thankful that despite his prior experience, he didn't put me down.)

One thing, however, has always had the power to turn me into a shaking, sweating bag of wobbly jelly: public speaking. To say I hate it would be a huge understatement. For me, it's everyone else's shark, dentist, spider, and mother-in-law rolled into one big ball of terror.

So that's why my being on stage in the San Francisco theater that night in front of fourteen hundred people is so crazy. I was a specialist in running away from stages at high speed. The times I did end up on them, I was a true Jedi Master at embarrassing myself. I have several such occasions to consider—all opportunities for me to shine that went south quickly.

"My name is Mustafa, and I am an exchange student from Southern Yemen."

That was how I started my college Human Resource Management class presentation. Introducing myself as a person I clearly was not, from a place I was not, to a group of people who already knew me. Why? If only I knew. It seemed like a good idea after taking down four bottles of Corona in quick succession before taking to the podium. Before the presentation, I had walked into a group meeting with a six-pack in hand—two of which were already empty—and proceeded to drink two more while prepping for my turn to speak my brilliant opening lines. When speech time came, the lecturer understandably didn't take kindly to my lighthearted approach and lightheaded comments. Don't get me wrong—I am no alcoholic and your intervention is unnecessary. Drinking just seemed like a good idea to relax my nerves before speaking to the class. Had I known then what I know now, I certainly would have quickly vetoed my own plan.

That year, my final year at one of Ireland's top schools, I received first-class honors in all subjects but one: Human Resource Management. Seventy percent was the magic number—it defined a first-class honor and was generally the highest mark one received at University College Dublin. My beer-soaked presentation had knocked me into a lower percentile and I graduated with a second-class honors degree. I felt bitter about it but only had myself to blame for my near miss. Damn fear of public speaking.

I took a year off to work and travel in Australia before returning to earn my master's degree. I selected the same course with the same lecturer in order to correct my mistake and do better the second time around. The lecturer certainly hadn't forgotten me or my terrible public speaking ability. For the second time running, she gave me the exact same grade. Again, it was her course that brought down my average, and that meant the difference between a first-class and a second-class honors degree. Essentially, in both my undergraduate degree and master's degree, I narrowly missed out on earning the highest level possible due to my fear of public speaking.

It didn't take long for my fear to worm its way into my new working life. I landed a job with the Irish government as a marketing executive, helping high-potential Irish startup companies expand in the United States.

The new recruits, myself included, had to present at a team get-together in New York. I had no beer available to calm my nerves this time. I also had nowhere to place the chart I had drawn to illustrate my main points to the assembled executives. As my nerves took hold, I frantically searched for the best section of wall to stick it to. One 4 × 4 framed section stood out. Perfect. I pulled a piece of duct tape and . . . "No!!!" I heard people suddenly scream. In my bumbling state, I had tried to stick my poster to a $40,000 piece of artwork that I didn't even notice. Some say I made a terrible first impression. By some, I mean everyone.

Several years later I found myself in Shanghai, China, the only Westerner working in China for Hult International Business School, the world's largest business school by enrollment. This sole-Westerner status, apparently, was enough to make me the ideal candidate to host the Asian leg of the Hult Prize, a global competition run in partnership with the Clinton Global Initiative. I actively tried to avoid it, but I needed the help of the organizer on another project, so I ultimately gave into the arm-twisting.

I was a nervous wreck as usual. As I took the stage, I had enough paper in hand to rival *War and Peace*. I stumbled through it terribly, relieved only by the knowledge that most of the assembled four-hundred-plus Chinese officials and participants had no idea how to comprehend an Irish accent. Of course, then I screwed up their Chinese names, too.

That certainly translated.

Three opportunities to improve my educational and professional standing, three tremendous failures that stemmed directly from my inability to stand in the front of a room and speak like a person. It didn't make any sense. It didn't fit with my personality. I wasn't a painfully shy guy. I was outgoing. I could hold a conversation with just about anyone and walk away seeming intelligent, competent, and capable of handling pointy utensils. But the second I was faced with a captive audience, I became a guy my friends jokingly referred to as "Shakin' Stevens." My alter ego sweated. He stammered. He shuddered. Sometimes he BYO-Corona'ed. You wouldn't trust Shakin' Stevens with a sharp fork, let alone a roomful of clients.

The time came to put an end to this sequence of embarrassment, but it was certainly not a decision I made on my own.

When my friend Arash suffered a severe spinal cord injury, I suggested organizing a comedy show and recruiting some top comedians to perform in order to raise funds for his continued physical therapy. As luck would have it, my old neighbor, Tim, was a headlining comedian and kindly agreed to do it. What I didn't anticipate was Arash's insistence that I host the event! He knew nothing of my fear of public speaking and had no idea just how bad I was at it. He just knew me as someone who was full of words in everyday life and scared of very little. There was no way that I could say no. To this point I would have described my fear of public speaking as crippling. A description that, in this moment, paled in comparison to the reality my friend was facing, and a more fearful, life-altering application of the word.

Knowing what I had gotten myself in for, I set out to learn all I could about stand-up comedy and public speaking before the event. Tim Ferriss is an author and entrepreneur who popularized the idea of "meta learning," learning a skill in the shortest amount of time possible. In *The 4-Hour Chef: The Simple Path to Cooking Like a Pro, Learning Anything, and Living the Good Life*, Ferriss deconstructed a skill he wanted to master into its most basic components and determined which of those components would give his ability the biggest boost. As a huge Tim Ferriss fan, I figured this would be a great way to raise the bar for my public speaking ability.

There was just one problem.

In *The 4-Hour Chef*, Ferriss opted to learn how to cook. It was something he wanted to do, not something that made him want to drop into the fetal position on the floor of his presumably very Zen kitchen. The idea of throwing myself headfirst into the ABCs of public speaking sounded terrible. There had to be another way, something else that I could learn that was aligned with public speaking but didn't make me want to flee to Japan with my bow and arrows to study *yabusame*. But what?

Stand-up comedy.

The idea of stand-up comedy rattled through my brain for just a second, but I heard it loud and clear. I liked to make people laugh and, provided that they were my friends and not an audience, I was pretty good at it. Stand-up put you on a stage. In front of people. To sink or swim or run off the platform in tears. Yes, stand-up would be my gateway skill.

I wondered if stand-up comedy could be broken down into processes aimed at mastery, as tested and popularized by Ferriss in his top-selling books. Could I use comedy to craft more memorable, engaging, and effective presentations for the audience without making myself want to die? What should I focus on in order to obtain the outcome I desired? What are comedians learning the hard way on stage, often through trial and error as they clock those ten thousand hours that author Malcolm Gladwell says make a master? How does someone who feels they are not naturally funny kill it on stage? By studying comedy and the processes stand-up comedians use, can we make our presentations and key messages stand out while overcoming fears of public speaking? Can this be done quickly?

I'd soon find out that the answer to all of these is "yes."

For one full year I became a comedian called "Irish Dave." Being from Ireland, I thought this was a stage name that seemed far too obvious to bestow on myself, but Americans seemed to like it, so I committed to being Irish Dave for a year. (How hard could it be? I was already Irish and already called Dave.) New comedians, due to lack of experience, find it hard to get bookings on paid shows, so I made it look like "Irish Dave" had been around doing comedy for a while, back in Ireland of course. I created a website, a Facebook fan page, you name it: Irish Dave, "He's big in Ireland"—a fact that surprisingly nobody questioned. Would "American Dave" make it big stateside? Probably not.

I am a keen kite surfer, and one day after a session under the Golden Gate Bridge, I told a fellow kite surfer my show-hosting predicament. As chance would have it, he was a comedian in his spare time and took it upon himself to organize my professional comedy debut. He contacted a booker friend, bending the truth ever so slightly by telling him I was a very funny comedian visiting from Ireland. Before I knew what was happening I was scheduled to perform for twenty minutes as part of a paid show. Twenty minutes! With the charity show for Arash looming, I agreed to take the stage. It was certainly baptism by fire but, amazingly, it wasn't so bad. I got a few laughs along the way and it was a huge improvement from my days as Mustafa from Southern Yemen, the Corona-fueled madman with Shakin' Stevens moves and occasional opinions on human resource management.

I decided I would keep the experiment going for a year, regardless of how the charity show went. I dedicated myself to applying the Pareto Principle (aka the 80/20 Principle, based on the concept that 80 percent of results come from 20 percent of the actions), which is to say that I would set about determining which set of actions to focus on to bring the greatest results. I would figure out what makes a joke funny, how to best craft and deliver it, and what comedians knew that business speakers did not. I have always walked the line between business and comedy in my own life, so this seemed like a great excuse to combine the two. If I could help a few others by documenting what I learned along the way, then the quest would be worth it.

I kept this experiment mostly to myself. I had just left a well-paying corporate job and was unsure of my next move. I didn't really want to worry my family by telling them I was about to put my time into becoming a stand-up comedian . . . temporarily, with no goal to be an actual full-time comedian. The next booked show I did was five ladies and me. The name of that show: "Estrogen Entrée with a Side of Balls"—yes, I was that side of balls. I could imagine the conversation with my father: "So . . . David, glad to see you have left your job to become a side of balls . . . Do you think you might go back to being employed anytime soon?"

Why the focus on comedy? Beyond the demands of my comfort level, what made me so sure that stand-up would help me become a better public speaker?

For one, because science says so. "The brain doesn't pay attention to boring things," notes biologist John Medina in his best-selling book *Brain Rules*. He writes that "emotionally charged" events like laughter trigger a dopamine release, which "greatly aids memory and information processing. You can think of it like a Post-it note that reads, 'Remember this!'"

Also, today's audience has been conditioned to receive info via humor. Thank Jon Stewart that people no longer watch *20/20* or *Nightline* for news. They want infotainment, not information.

Carmine Gallo is a news anchor turned author, columnist, and keynote speaker. In short, he's a guy people actually want to listen to. He says humor is one of the nine key elements in successful TED talks that are "scientifically proven to increase the likelihood that your pitch or presentation will be successful, whether you're pitching to one person or speaking to thousands." It also "lowers defenses, making your audience more receptive to your message."[1]

As we will see later in the book, there are several TED talks that produce more laughs per minute than the classic comedy *The Hangover*. Needless to say they are also a lot more informative. At the time of writing, every one of the ten most popular TED talks moves the humor needle.

Top speakers, savvy startups, leading ad agencies, and Fortune 500 firms alike are turning to humor as the ultimate tool for being memorable amidst the ringtones, vibrations, and swipe-rights of modern life, and you should be, too. Great speakers know this. Every time I watch effective business speakers, I see the same techniques used by stand-up comedians at work. If the goal is improved public speaking, stand-up comedy offers a solid means of achieving it.

> **If the goal is improved public speaking, stand-up comedy offers a solid means of achieving it.**

Darren LaCroix, who brings incredible stories and captivating humor to conferences around the globe, says he was "born without a funny bone in his body," but touts himself as living proof that humor is a skill that can be learned. A self-proclaimed "student of comedy," he applies that humor to public speaking. In 2001, Darren out-spoke twenty-five thousand contestants from fourteen countries to win the coveted title of World Champion of Public Speaking (yes, they exist).

According to Darren, there are three keys to public speaking success: "stage time, stage time, and stage time."

Open mic nights offer a perfect opportunity for inexperienced speakers to perform for a small audience, and they run nightly in all major cities. In New York City, it is not uncommon for an aspiring comedian to go on stage more than four times in one night. Most professional comedians will tell you that, to make a living from comedy, it takes around seven years. Many average four hours a day honing their craft—including writing, practicing, watching other comedians, and performing. Four hours a day means many dedicated comedians invest roughly 1,460 hours of time each year to improving their skills, adding up to over ten thousand hours in a seven-year period. If stage time is the key to making it as a keynote, then adhering to even a fraction of the stand-up comedian's practice schedule is a smart move.

Most comedians will invest an estimated twenty-two hours of work for every minute of a one-hour special show (normally produced yearly). As business speakers, we don't need sixty minutes. Even one minute's worth of comedy—with four to five laughs taken and spread out over a nine-minute business talk—will make you much funnier (and more effective) than 90 percent of business speakers out there, because most speakers and presentations are boring! Most should come with a pillow, a warm glass of milk, and a Snuggie!

My time with the Irish government and financial services company PricewaterhouseCoopers combined to make me one of the most well-rested men in Ireland. Because most presentations are glorified snooze-fests, long keynotes are becoming a thing of the past. Who has an hour to focus on one person? Most people switch off at around the ten-minute mark. As John Medina references in *Brain Rules*, studies by noted educator Wilbert McKeachie demonstrate that "typically, attention increases from the beginning of the lecture to ten minutes into the lecture and decreases after that point." This is why many TED talks are now shorter than ten minutes.

They figured out that brevity is levity.

And they're not the first to have discovered this. Some of the best speeches in history have clocked in at under ten minutes. Abraham Lincoln's Gettysburg Address was 272 words and lasted less than three minutes; Winston Churchill's "Blood, Toil, Tears and Sweat" speech was 688 words and just over five minutes. The most powerful emotional expression two humans can say to each other is just three words: "I," "love," and "*cake*."

Stand-up comedy, at its basic principles, is a combination of material (what you say) and delivery (how you say it). It is no different than typical speeches or presentations. TV slots for new comedians tend to be under five minutes, which forces them to continuously refine and refine and refine again in order to get maximum impact from each word. There is a saying in comedy that "a tight five is better than a sloppy fifteen." Yet business presentations worldwide fail to abide by the same principle. Instead, there tends to be a lot of sloppy fifteens. Why? The necessary stage time, structure, and conscious editing for maximum impact just aren't there—most people don't have to speak often enough to get it. Conversely, the speakers who deliver their talk most tend to be the best and most polished. They know where the laugh lines are, they know what phrasing works best, and they know their timing. Just like stand-up comedians.

Since the crash of 2008, employment markets and popular perspectives on how work should be have fundamentally shifted. The loyalty that comes from long-term employers and single-company careers is gone. People no longer stand for their company because they have little faith that their company will stand for them. To be safe, and indeed to prosper in this economy, what you can do and who you are need to be transferable; what you did and whom you did it for doesn't really matter anymore.

As Reid Hoffman, the founder of LinkedIn, says, it's time for *The Start-Up of You*. It's time, as author James Altucher says, to *Choose Yourself*. To do this you need to market yourself—whether you like it or not—just as Tim Ferriss, the *4-Hour Chef* author who inspired me, has done so successfully. A big part of this is taking every opportunity to tell your story. Tim, as it happens, is no fan of public speaking either. What does he have to say about it? "If you're getting chased by a lion, you don't need to run faster than the lion, just the people running with you. Speaking with other people is similar: you don't need to be perfect, you just need to be better than a few others."[2]

Learning from stand-up comedy can give us a huge advantage in building our public speaking ability by providing the tools to help us not only outrun the lion, but leave him laughing in our dust. And that is the premise of this book. That is what I'm going to show you: how to use comedy techniques to transform your public speaking, and by doing so, help make the world a lot more entertaining for everybody.

In one year, I went from being deeply afraid of public speaking to being able to headline a stand-up comedy show, host a business conference and charity event, and speak at multiple business gatherings. For one full year, I performed as Irish Dave, the "accomplished" comedian, in several hundred shows across all of Northern California's top comedy clubs. I also interviewed several hundred comedians, performers, and public speaking experts and read every book, quote, and guru I could find on the topic. I broke the techniques down, applied the 80/20 Principle (thanks, Pareto), and performed a series of experiments on yours truly to determine the seven key principles, or habits, that brought forth the biggest outcome. I explain these seven key principles in this book. I explore each of the seven comedy habits in its own chapter in detail and follow them with a series of short exercises to apply the learning.

Some of you just grimaced like a bulldog chewing a wasp. Exercises? Don't worry! They are easy and based on what's worked in teaching these concepts to thousands of people. (There is a free workbook to accompany this book, available at http://7comedyhabits.com/workbook). You can get just the tips at any time by going to the Tipliography section (yes, I did invent that word) in the back of the book. It's like a bibliography, only useful, and of course, spelled differently. These are seven principles and a host of tips that would have saved me a lot of time and embarrassment if I had only known them earlier. Trust me, if I could defeat Shakin' Stevens, you can get over your own fears, too.

My year of study and self-experimentation brought me to three conclusions:

1. Top business speakers are using humor.
2. They are developing laugh lines using the same process as comedians, even though most are unaware of it.
3. You don't need to be naturally funny to get laughs. Most comedians I met were not.

To be honest, I still have a fear of public speaking. The difference now is it's manageable. I have a tried and tested array of stories and funny anecdotes I know will initiate one of the most powerful forces available to mankind: laughter.

"I am from Ireland so I do have a bit of an accent. If I say something funny and you guys don't laugh, I'm going to assume you didn't understand and just say it again."

I still use this line—in fact, I have used it many times—and it always gets a laugh. Developed in comedy clubs and at open mic nights, it's the same line I use when speaking in a business environment, and it's one of many. It follows a structure and a methodology that, when combined with six other habits, will make you a funnier speaker and make your fear of public speaking a thing of the past.

This is not a magic book. Simply reading these seven principles won't make you instantly funnier, more successful, or more attractive. Add a little practice, however, and it just might.

#1
Start with a Story

"Stories are the creative conversion of life itself into a more powerful, clearer, more meaningful experience. They are the currency of human contact."

—Robert McKee

I woke in the middle of the night to a series of loud rumbling noises. My location was a small, windowless room in volcanic Guatemala. I was twenty-five years old and had just moved in with a local family as part of a Spanish language school home-stay program. Unfortunately for me, the epicenter of this rumbling was my stomach, and the cause was food poisoning. And, as I was about to find out, it was a very bad dose. While I was curled up in the throes of intestinal anarchy, my host family was in the next room, completely unaffected by the gut-twisting superbug. The projectile vomiting started twenty minutes later and seemed to have no stop. With no windows, no trashcan, and no time to react, my backpack loaded with clothes bore the brunt of the storm, with the floor and walls coming a close second and third. I heard footsteps coming to check on me.

My host mother, Flor, a robust lady in traditional long, local dress, came rushing in to find me covered in puke and her whitewashed walls looking like fifty shades of green. I wasn't due to start classes until the following day, so at this point my Spanish was nonexistent. I rummaged through my sodden belongings to find a small pocket dictionary and flipped to the health section. I looked her in the eyes with my most pitiful puppy-dog-meets-drowned-rat face and, pointing to my source of wisdom, read aloud, "Vomitando . . . Vomitando aquí," as I pointed to my bag; "aquí," the floor; and, "aquí también," ("here as well") as I gave the walls a broad stroking.

"Alcohólico de Irlanda," she mumbled, assuming incorrectly that my culture and not her local dish had gotten the better of me.

Tell a Story to Teach

Thankfully, my condition and my Spanish improved quickly. I never forgot the Spanish word for "vomiting," and I suspect you won't, either. Experiences do that to you, and stories—shared experiences—do that, too. For better or worse our brains are hardwired to recognize, remember, and appreciate the information that comes to us through storytelling. Stories help us learn.

Rapid language acquisition experts like Benny Lewis (a fellow Irishman) also stress the use of mnemonic devices. Defined as "any learning technique that aids information retention," mnemonics aim to translate information into a form that the brain can retain better than its original form. Benny has a great example with learning the Spanish word *caber*, which means "to fit." *Caber* sounds like two words more familiar to native English speakers, *cab* and *bear*. Utilizing mnemonic devices, we can construct a short visual story of a bear trying to fit into a taxicab. To best remember it, you visualize the unlikely scenario in your mind in as much detail as possible. The premise of this idea is based on something scientists have known for a long time: the mind learns in stories and visual cues. Benny speaks twelve languages, and he learned them all in less time than it took me to learn basic commands *en Español*.

"The human species thinks in metaphors and learns through stories."
–Mary Catherine Bateson

Thus, one of the reasons for using stories in our speeches is that stories help us learn and remember things. We all want our audience to learn something and remember what we said.

Many of us have been to a comedy club and laughed hysterically at the comedian, but struggle to remember his/her name or what exactly was said. We've had the same experience with business speakers. When someone delivers information as a series of facts or opinions, it's hard for our brains to recall them.

Don't be that person. Our aim as public speakers is to be more memorable and have our audience spread our message for us. The best way to do this is to make it work the way the brain likes it—by wrapping the information in a story.

Tell a Story to Build Your Brand

Stories are great for memory retention, but there's another reason to tell a story: it connects you with and humanizes your brand.

Consider the origin of the word *brand*. It comes from a hot piece of metal people use to mark cows. True brands tell the world a very simple story, like, "This is Dave's cow." The job of the other kind of brand is much the same: to influence what people think of when they think of you. Stories are great for that. They give people's brains a thing to connect you with. They do the job marketers are supposed to be doing by giving people something to think of when they think of you. Yet much of the marketing industry still thinks it can get away with calling colors, typefaces, and canned music "branding." If those things are elements of a story, great. But without a story? That's just a random cow.

Ann Handley is a content marketer who inspires an entire industry. When it comes to storytelling, she says, "Some brands are doing it really well, but storytelling is not a skill marketers have necessarily needed over the last few decades."[3] In an article by Harrison Monarth in the *Harvard Business Review*, Johns Hopkins researcher Keith Quesenberry discusses the effectiveness of commercials that are like "mini movies." He says, "People are attracted to stories, because we're social creatures and we relate to other people."[4]

You may not be in marketing, but when you get up to make a speech, you are selling your content, your idea, and maybe even your cow. So you, too, need to develop your storytelling skills to better sell yourself. Whether your experiences tell how you disgusted your host family in Guatemala or how you led your company out of disaster, the same basic principles apply. You are always telling a story.

While most eight-year-olds were learning how to properly squeeze a lemon, Gary Vaynerchuk was managing seven lemonade stands across his neighborhood in Edison, New Jersey, his new home after moving with his family from Belarus. This kind of hustle has led him to numerous business successes, best-selling books, and TV appearances, and has edged him a few steps closer to his goal of buying the New York Jets football team. He is also one of the best business speakers out there and no stranger to using humor. Says Vaynerchuk, "Quality storytelling always wins. Always."[5]

It does not take long to find a compelling example. Airbnb went from a failing startup to a billion-dollar business built on a compelling story that their founders have become masters of telling. Airbnb started in 2007, when Joe Gebbia and Brian Chesky were struggling to pay their rent. There was a design conference coming to San Francisco and the city's hotels were fully booked, so they came up with the idea of renting out three airbeds on their living room floor and cooking breakfast for their guests. The site Airbedandbreakfast.com (later shortened to Airbnb) officially launched on August 11, 2008, and initially struggled. With no seed money, the founders hustled to self-fund and keep their dreams alive. They fell back on their design schooling and created special-edition breakfast cereals that capitalized on the presidential election: "Obama O's" (The Breakfast of Change) and "Cap'n McCains." The two sold 800 boxes of the cereal (priced at $40 each) in two months, making $30,000 in profits for the cash-strapped founders.

The reasons why they started Airbnb, combined with the fact that they kept the idea alive with breakfast cereal, made a compelling and memorable story for Joe and Brian to tell. It showed their idea was a solution to a real problem, that they were passionate about it, and that they were willing to do anything to succeed.

Investor Paul Graham was impressed with Gebbia and Chesky's hustle and decided to take on Airbnb in his Y Combinator program (an American seed accelerator providing early stage funding and advice for startups), even though he initially didn't like their idea. They went on to raise multiple rounds of investment with top-tier firms and VCs and, in April 2014, they closed a round based on a valuation of approximately $10 billion.

Seth Godin is a prolific writer, blogger, and very often hilarious public speaker. He is the author of several notable marketing books, such as *Purple Cow, Small Is the New Big*, and *Permission Marketing*, and his ideas have been referenced, regurgitated, and repackaged by just about everyone. Expanding on Godin's idea that "marketing is no longer about the stuff that you make, but about the stories you tell," Actionable Marketing Guide blogger Heidi Cohen writes, "In the social media age, your company must build the best product you can because customers will talk about your products and services on social media platforms and in real life. Products need stories to provide context and human emotion. They provide the beginning, middle, and end."[6]

Airbnb gave people a great story that clearly explained who the company was, defined the values it held, and directly addressed the needs of those it was trying to serve. For their community of loyal users, Joe and Brian were striving to provide an experience, a home, and a sense of belonging that people don't get from traditional hotels. Their story also saved them a lot of marketing dollars as media and user attention spread their tale far and wide. The hotel industry had a new competitor, and this competitor had creativity, passion, hustle, and a story worth telling. People don't invest in your business or product. They invest in you and your story. If you want people to remember what you say, tell a compelling story.

> People don't invest in your business or product. They invest in you and your story. If you want people to remember what you say, tell a compelling story.

"Storytelling is everything," says Barbara Corcoran from ABC-TV's *Shark Tank*. "Show me an MBA and your sales numbers, that's fine. But tell me a great story about how you got started and your vision, and we'll talk."[7]

The same logic could easily be applied to stand-up comedy. Jokes that tell a story, that immerse the audience into the scenario, are much more likely to get them to invest and laugh along.

How to Craft Your Story

So how do we craft a great story? Whether it's business or not, the story always needs a personal element. Make it your own. Audiences respond better to a story that features the storyteller. Include stories from your own life experiences before referencing those of others. Nobody knows your stories better than you, which also makes telling them a lot easier. Remember, better public speaking is the goal here, and stand-up comedy is our means of achieving it.

The best way to be more engaging, memorable, and funny quickly is to tell a story that contains a few essential elements. "Who wants what and what stops them from getting it?" This, according to Golden Globe–winning writer and three-time Emmy nominee Bill Grundfest, is the secret sauce of all stories in its most simplified form. Yet what makes stories great is the detail we add. We need to put meat on the bones of our story by including the following elements:

Have a hero/protagonist.

Decide who will be the central character of the story. Often people remember the characters more than the story itself. Loose contenders so far in mine are Shakin' Stevens, Mustafa, and some experimental comedian called Irish Dave.

Describe what your hero is up against.

What challenges does the character have to overcome? What do they want and what is stopping them from getting it? This can be as feisty as Guatemalan food or as terrifying as public speaking. This is your story's source of tension.

Build in a specific transcending emotion.

You need something that breaks down barriers; love, lust, greed, passion, and loss are perfect.

Include a clear lesson or transformation.

Make sure your characters move toward their goal, objective, or solution to a problem. Even if it's just finding a bathroom, or omitting words without laying an egg.

Add twists and turns to the story.

Try not to make it predictable for the listener. Introduce a question or challenge and don't be too quick to solve it.

Make it believable.

It is essential that your story allows the listener to suspend their disbelief by listening to what you are saying rather than questioning the truth of your words. Vulnerability and jokes at your own expense work well here. Tell people how you really felt. Leave some of yourself on the stage. If something was scary, nobody wants to hear how confident you were in overcoming it. If your hands were like a partially defrosted mackerel, tell them.

Have a clear incident that makes the story really take off.

Often referred to as the *inciting incident,* it is a concept popularized by the master of story, Robert McKee, in his famed three-day "Story Seminar" given all over the world. It is described by Steven Pressfield, author of *The Legend of Bagger Vance* and *The War of Art,* here: "The inciting incident in a screenplay or novel is that event that gets the story rolling. In *The Hangover,* it's the moment when the guys wake up in their trashed villa with no memory of what happened the night before—and realize that they've lost their friend Doug. With that, the story kicks into gear. Everything before that is just setup . . . Ask yourself of your project, 'What is the inciting incident?' 'When does the "story" take off?' You'd be surprised how many would-be novels/screenplays/restaurants/startups don't have inciting incidents. That's why they don't work."[8]

Know where you want to end up (the punch line) from the outset.

The last line should be the first line you write. Then work backward toward your inciting incident and setup.

Quickly build in a hook to grab your audience's attention and draw them into the story.

This is especially important in light of today's ever-decreasing attention spans. You're your audience's reason to keep their phones in their pockets. For instance, what happened at the Castro Theatre that night? For someone afraid of public speaking, standing in front of fourteen hundred people doesn't sound like the best plan. If you're wondering if I'll get back to that, don't worry. I will.

Reference your opening lines/setup in the conclusion of your story.

This is referred to as the Bookend Technique, and it will give your story a feeling of completion or symmetry. More on this in chapter seven.

Frame your story within a three-act structure.

The three acts are Setup (Beginning), Confrontation (Middle), and Resolution (End).

The hook and inciting incident usually happen within the first act. "People have forgotten how to tell a story," said Steven Spielberg. "Stories don't have a middle or an end anymore. They usually have a beginning that never stops beginning."[9] If one of the most awarded directors of all time says that's a problem, it's a problem. Make sure you don't make the same mistake.

Entertain.

Modern-day storytelling is joke telling. Today's audiences expect some lightheartedness and entertainment. Airbnb gave it to them in the form of funky-named cereals. A story should make people care by including personal experience that the audience can relate to their own lives. The most powerful stories are not about the storyteller; they are about the person who is hearing the story. Most marketers and presenters forget this.

Sometimes, being entertaining doesn't even require you to tell jokes. In his book, *Talk Like TED: The 9 Public-Speaking*

Secrets of the World's Top Minds, Carmine Gallo reminds us, "The funny thing about humor is that you don't need to tell a joke to get a laugh." It can be enough simply not to take yourself too seriously—or to be brutally honest.

This has rung very true for my own attempts at being funny on stage. Often the biggest laughs came from stories and encounters I had in my own life rather than cleverly crafted witticisms or opinions—my *vomitando* story has served up more laughs than any alliterative quip I could come up with. The world is a funny place and your existence within it is probably funnier. Accepting that fact is a blessing that gives you everything you need to see humor and craft stories on a daily basis. All you have to do is document them and then tell someone.

"The safest humor involves personal stories, because they are guaranteed to be original and unheard, they can be practiced and perfected, and they are highly personalized to your style."
–Alan Weiss

The Art of Storytelling

On a windswept, summer-like evening in San Francisco in May 2014, I go to check out The Moth storytelling series, founded by novelist George Dawes Green. Since its launch in 1997, the series has presented thousands of stories, each of them told live and without notes to standing-room-only crowds worldwide. It has a great mix of performers, authors, business speakers, and everyday folks. In short, it is the perfect development ground for TED-type talks. High-profile storytellers have included

Malcolm Gladwell, Salman Rushdie, John Turturro, Annie Proulx, Gabriel Byrne, and AJ Jacobs. Not-so-high-profile storytellers include . . . some Irish guy who's definitely not Gabriel Byrne.

The format is quite harrowing for anyone afraid of public speaking the way I am. You sign up, but there is no guarantee you will be called to tell a story. There are ten spots available and, most of the time, more than ten storytellers sign up. Names are drawn at random live on stage. At the insistence of my friends, I put my name in the hat, figuring I would let fate decide whether I appeared. Names are called immediately before you are expected to take the stage—you don't know the order or even if you will be called—so there is little to do but wait.

The room is packed, and although the air conditioning blows with an arctic chill, I am sweating uncontrollably. Thankfully, I have learned to wear dark colors to hide the sweaty spots. After all, showing your humanity is important, but that doesn't mean it needs to be sweaty.

Humanity, in fact, is one of the keys to great storytelling and great stand-up. One of The Moth's great storytellers, the *New Yorker* writer Adam Gopnik, makes a distinction between good storytellers and good stories in that same light:

> A good storyteller is somebody who's comfortable on his or her feet and is enough of a ham to get a charge out of the response of a crowd, that surge of electricity that goes back and forth between you and an audience. If that does not turn you on you won't be a good storyteller. A good story has to be extremely particular and peculiar to your life. It has to have an element of singularity and yet—and this is the alchemy and paradox of storytelling—it has to be something immediately universal, part of something that we all experience.[10]

As a good storyteller, you need to be totally human. Be vulnerable, embrace embarrassment, and vocalize failure before success. This was something stand-up comedian and Moth storyteller Mike Birbiglia tapped into when he described his first impressions of "making out" in high school: "It was like watching a dog eating spaghetti." He thought kissing seemed weird, so he never tried it. But he told all his friends that he had. When it finally did happen, he says, "It was like eating the spaghetti and the fork." He later recounts how, after his first make-out, the girl told his friends that he was a terrible kisser—an embarrassing public rejection, a universal fear that everyone has probably felt at some point in their lives. Rather than admit his inexperience, the true reason why he was "the worst kisser she's ever kissed," Mike tried to save face in front of his buddies: "Yeah, that sounds about right. I'm a terrible kisser. That's kind of my thing."[11] This is the essence of human nature and what people want to hear. They are quite happy to hear what a fool you have been before opening up to your success, and happier still if you never achieve it.

So as I sit in The Moth audience, with name after name drawn from the hat and read aloud by the host, Dhaya, who looks every bit the consummate stage professional, my nerves are multiplying with every passing second. Focusing on someone else's story seems near impossible when fate has you on the clock. Storytellers come and go in agonizing slow motion. Maybe tonight I'll be off the hook. Nine speakers have taken the stage and told their stories in front of a packed audience of strangers, while I am left sitting nervously cycling uncontrollably between hot and cold. Then finally, "Next to the stage, please give a warm welcome to our final storyteller, David Nihill."

I am a bag of jelly by this point but keep my nerves in check by remembering one of the greatest things about storytelling: the story is yours. You know it better than anyone. You don't have to train yourself to remember it. You have told it before to friends, family, or colleagues, whether at work, a dinner party, or some informal setting. You have done this before.

I start to relax once I am on stage. The previously intimidating crowd seems to blend into one friendly sea of faces. These people don't want to see me fail—most people don't. Ultimately people want to see other people do well and will cheer them on, especially if they connect or relate to them. Starting with a story gives you the best chance of doing this. Especially a story about yourself that you know. So I tell a story about my time living in Shanghai. It is my own. I know it better than anyone because it happened to me. And as I settle into my storytelling, I can feel my connection with my audience. My laugh lines hit, and people are nodding their heads in recognition as my little slice of the human experience connected to theirs. When the crowd applauds loudly, I know it's over. Outscoring all the others, I have won.

The good folks behind The Moth are true experts in the art of the story. Below are some of their best tips for storytellers, from novice to expert:[12]

Be forewarned: stories are told, not read.

We love how the storyteller connects with the audience when there is no PAGE between them! Please know your story "by heart" but not by rote memorization. No notes, paper, or cheat sheets allowed on stage.

Have some stakes.

Stakes are essential in live storytelling. What do you stand to gain or lose? Why is what happens in the story important to you? If you can't answer this, then think of a different story. A story without stakes is an essay and is best experienced on the page, not the stage.

Start in the action.

Have a great first line that sets up the stakes or grabs attention.

No: "So I was thinking about climbing this mountain. But then I watched a little TV and made a snack and took a nap and my mom called and vented about her psoriasis then I did a little laundry (a whites load) (I lost another sock, darn it!) and then I thought about it again and decided I'd climb the mountain the next morning."

Yes: "The mountain loomed before me. I had my hunting knife, some trail mix, and snow boots. I had to make it to the little cabin and start a fire before sundown or freeze to death for sure."

Steer clear of meandering endings.

They kill a story! Your last line should be clear in your head before you start. Yes, bring the audience along with you as you contemplate what transpires in your story, but remember, you are driving the story and must know the final destination. Keep your hands on the wheel!

Know your story well enough so you can have fun!

Watching you panic to think of the next memorized line is harrowing for the audience. Make an outline, memorize your bullet points, and play with the details. Enjoy yourself. Imagine you are at a dinner party, not a deposition.

I followed these tips when I told my story and I did something else: I made it funny. In fact, the biggest advantage my story had over the other nine on that windy San Francisco night was this: it was funnier. The Moth won't tell you that your story has to be funny, but those that incorporate some humor always do very well. I have now won a number of storytelling nights and performed alongside some of the biggest names nationally, and humor always plays as big a part in my stories as it does in my victories. In the next chapter we'll look more at adding humor to your stories.

Whether you're a stand-up comedian, budding storyteller, or a substandard Spanish language student involuntarily destroying a Guatemalan home, your story matters, and how you tell it makes all the difference in how it will be received. Combining storytelling, humanity, and laughter will give you a huge advantage in your public speaking, and the odds are good that you already have all the raw material you need. After all, we all have had something funny happen to us at some stage in life—now it's just a matter of making it funny on an actual stage.

Exercise: Start Your Funny Story File

Think back through your experiences and make a bullet-point list of stories you like that have happened to you or your friends. When you are in the company of your friends and family, what stories do you like to tell? Think fun over funny at this stage. You can also pull material from your favorite books—the odds are in your favor that most people have not even read the biggest bestsellers, so this is an easy source.

Consider travel, school, college, parties, work, interaction with parents/in-laws, customer, and client interactions. Looking at old photos will help to jog memories. We all have had something funny or embarrassing happen to us at some point and, as Birbiglia showed us, even if it wasn't funny then, it might be funny now. As Charlie Chaplin said, sometimes "to truly laugh, you must be able to take your pain, and play with it."

We want to identify topics you already know well and already like to talk about. This will make your on-stage delivery much more engaging. Imagine your best friend, partner, or coworker completing this sentence: "(Your name here) is always talking about . . ." These are the beginnings of your story list, which we will edit as we go forward through the book.

Often listening to other people's stories will jog your own memory. With this in mind, buy tickets to a comedy or storytelling show and go see it this week, or listen to a podcast like The Moth, Risk, Mortified, or Snap Judgment. Remember, great stories often come from seemingly mundane topics.

#2 Add Humor—Find the Funny

"The end of laughter is followed by the
height of listening."

—Jeffrey Gitomer

In 2000, I was lucky enough to spend a summer on a work and travel program in the United States with a group of other Irish students. The original plan was to live in Boston, but, faced with a shortage of temporary housing at the time, we ended up in Hampton Beach, New Hampshire. Not quite the intellectual landscape of MIT and Harvard, but that wasn't going to stop our good time. We quickly embraced the state motto, "Live free or die," and set about having as much fun as possible in our new surroundings: freely living it up, pushing our boundaries, and hoping that we didn't die.

Then one day my neighbor handed me a beer bong. It had never before occurred to me to drink beer through a funnel. Frankly, I didn't see the point. As a culture, we Irish love a drink way too much to shoot it down our throats through a tube. Plus, Ireland only has one drinking game—it's called life.

"Call me old-fashioned," I said to my neighbor, looking at the outstretched funnel in his hands, "but a pint glass works just fine."

"That's fine. If you're not up for it, you don't have to."

My eyes narrowed as my competitive streak kicked in. Ireland doesn't win an awful lot in sports, but we are undefeated in the pursuit of Pyrrhic victories.

"Give me the funnel."

Twelve funneled beers later, I finally bowed out. Now, anyone familiar with drinking beer from a funnel knows exactly what I looked like at this point and exactly where I was heading. It wasn't long before the shout "Hampton Police, open the door!" came, as a fist on the other side of our apartment door knocked loudly. I'd seen the cultural masterpiece that is *Cops*, which even ran in Ireland, so I knew they needed a warrant to come in. With the funnel in one hand, I politely pulled back the curtain that covered the door and gave them a friendly wave.

The door flew open abruptly. Turns out, *Cops* was not an accurate representation of police protocol.

"Where's the guy in the gray shirt?" the officer shouted as he stepped forward menacingly. *Oh shit,* I thought, *that guy is screwed.*

Looking down, I realize that *I* am the guy in the gray shirt. *Oh shit.*

And that's when the audience really laughs. The moment I realize that I'm the one the cops are looking for is one of my proven laugh lines. It's a story I have told many times to friends and family, and I know where they will likely laugh.

Now that we understand the importance of crafting a good story and the ingredients involved in doing so, we need to look at adding humor. I mentioned in chapter one how my story at The Moth was funnier than all the others. Why? I had told it before in front of the most difficult kind of audience there is: those looking up at me on a stand-up comedy stage. As Jerry Seinfeld says, "No one is more judged in civilized society than a stand-up comedian. Every twelve seconds you're rated."

When you first tell a story at an open mic or on a comedy stage, you are forced to cut out the unnecessary pieces and tighten it up. You rapidly learn where the laugh lines are and how to get to them as quickly as possible. Great business speakers do the same thing. The only way to learn where your best laugh lines are is through trial and error, but when you hit on one you will remember it. Your audience's laughter burns a mental Post-it note in your mind because it feels good to make people laugh.

When asked whether they would like to be funnier, most people say they would. Who wouldn't? Everybody loves a good joke. It helps us in every walk of life, both personally and professionally. Those who use humor connect more deeply, build better relationships, increase personal productivity, earn more, motivate more effectively, get referred more, are more memorable, stand out, and have more fun!

"A sense of humor is part of the art of leadership, or getting along with people, of getting things done," said Dwight D. Eisenhower.[13] As Martha Craumer wrote in the *Harvard Communication Letter*, "People who use [humor], particularly in stressful or seemingly one-down positions, are viewed as being on top of things, being in charge and in control, whether they are in fact or not."[14]

In their best-selling book, *Multipliers*, Liz Wiseman and Greg McKeown describe how they found that nearly every great manager has a great sense of humor. A good salesperson, marketer, community manager, leader, or business development manager needs to know how to create a connection, and the fastest way of doing that is by making someone laugh.

21

Even if you're not a manager, it can help you in your job, starting with gaining employment: 98 percent of CEOs prefer job candidates with a sense of humor.[15] That said, when I told my old boss that I had more chance of getting myself pregnant than becoming an expert in nanotechnology, aerospace, and photonics (the three sectors she had me down to advise clients on), she spent the rest of the year trying to get me fired. She was the 2 percent. On a more positive note, 84 percent of those CEOs think that candidates with a sense of humor do better work.[16] (She was also the 16 percent.)

Having a sense of humor also makes you look more attractive in the dating pool. Recent data from online dating site eHarmony found that neither men nor women are interested in boring people. Site users listed "I must have someone who is sharp and can enjoy the humorous side of life" as their most important Must Have.

If you are single, unemployed, and reading this, then a bulb should be going off around now.

Andrew Tarvin is an international project manager turned humor engineer and TEDx speaker. Through his company, Humor That Works, Andrew teaches people how to be more productive, less stressed, and happier by using humor. In his words, "Humor is a competitive advantage. All of the companies stuck in the old mindset that work is work and shouldn't be fun are getting left in the dust by the companies who embrace a fundamental truth: their employees are humans, and humans respond to humor."[17]

How far can a good collection of funny stories and humor get you?

When asked during the 1984 presidential debates if, at seventy-three, he was too old to be president, Ronald Reagan quipped, "I will not make age an issue of this campaign. I am not going to exploit, for political purposes, my opponent's youth and inexperience."[18] The line, a timeless example of Reagan's sense of humor, even roused a laugh from his Democratic opponent, Walter Mondale. The Republican actor-turned-statesman and famed storyteller won reelection in the most lopsided victory in the history of American presidential politics.

> "The human race has only one really effective weapon and that is laughter."
> **–Mark Twain**

People love a funny story. As our good friend science tells us, we are wired to appreciate it. We are wired to love laughter. Our brains make this so by releasing dopamine. Dopamine feels awesome, so by making your audience laugh during your presentation or speaking event, you can actually make your audience feel good, giving your speech a natural, endorphin-fueled evolutionary advantage over those who opted for a typical, boring business presentation.

The most powerful thing you can do in comedy and in public speaking is deliver material that both you and your audience can connect to. What stories do you like to tell? What embarrassing and funny things do you typically talk about when in relaxed company? What mistakes have you made in your life that once were painful but now you are okay talking about?

According to comedian Ricky Gervais, "You should write about what you know because people can connect to it more easily." If you don't know what you are talking about, you cannot expand on it, go deep into the topic, and play with it like you actually care about it. If you don't care about it, nobody else will, either. But if you connect well with it, then your audience can as well.

"The whole object of comedy is to be yourself and the closer to that you get, the funnier you will be."
—Jerry Seinfeld

Comedian, writer, and actress Rita Rudner has the longest-running solo comedy show in Las Vegas. When explaining comedy on an episode of *RuPaul's Drag Race*, she says, "There's nothing funny about a confident person who's doing well." Rita's explanation links well to the often-quoted words of American television personality, writer, and comedian Steve Allen, speaking about the origins of comedic material:

> When I explained to a friend recently that the subject matter of most comedy is tragic (drunkenness, overweight, financial problems, accidents, etc.) he said, "Do you mean to tell me that the dreadful events of the day are a fit subject for humorous comment?" The answer is "No, but they will be pretty soon."
>
> Man jokes about the things that depress him, but he usually waits till a certain amount of time has passed . . . I guess you can make a mathematical formula out of it. Tragedy plus time equals comedy.[19]

Go back and complete the exercise at the end of the last chapter now if you have not done so. You need to build a story list to work with. Remember, this is not a magic book. It requires action. The laughs will be worth the work.

In a storytelling night, social event, or written long-form piece, there is time and space for lots of details and really painting a picture. At a business event or presentation, there is not. As speakers and presenters, we are on the clock, and the stories we tell can't take precedent over the information we are there to deliver. Stories are the method with which we deliver the important stuff. The more entertaining you can be, the more time you earn from your audience to be serious.

Often it works to simply listen and repeat. "Many funny things are said and done in your presence that are wholly original and can be used as a humorous illustration in your stories or speech," says Pat Hazell, one of the original writers for NBC's *Seinfeld*, a *Tonight Show* veteran, and declared by Showtime to be one of the five funniest people in America. "I overheard my kids arguing during a candy exchange after Halloween that was a wonderful message about value in negotiations. My oldest son Tucker said, 'I hate dark chocolate!' To which his brother responded, 'It's still candy, you got to respect that.' I use the dialogue verbatim because it is so pure and to the point."

Another great example of this comes from multiple *New York Times* best-selling author Jon Acuff. Jon is one of the best business speakers I have ever heard, perfectly lacing his talks with humor. Opening up a recent keynote to a packed conference, Jon spoke about how fast the world is changing:

One night at dinner my daughter said, "Dad, today at school the internet was down. We had to do everything . . . old fashioned." And I said, "Old fashioned, what does that mean?" and she said, "Well we were supposed to draw the state flag of Tennessee, but we couldn't Google it up, so we had to walk to the library . . . and look it up in a book." And I said, "With your legs? The whole way?"

Jeanne Robertson stands six-foot-two, but she is anything but intimidating. Specializing in hilarious stories based on her life experiences, Jeanne is an award-winning humorist, member of the National Speakers Association's Hall of Fame, and recipient of Toastmasters International's Golden Gavel award (a big deal in the world of public speaking).

According to Jeanne, "Humor is *not* about one-liners or being able to tell jokes. It's about accepting things about yourself that can't be changed and finding the humor in situations around you. Things happen on a daily basis that are really funny, but people often let the funny stuff get away, either because they don't notice it as funny, or they don't make it a priority to look for it."[20]

We are going to prioritize looking for it, then hone it down and punch it up.

Just like my unfortunate drinking challenge in New Hampshire, the process of adding humor to your stories involves a funnel—only one with much less potential for getting arrested.

The Joke Funnel

The Joke Funnel means we start as wide as we can to make our story relatable and relevant to the audience, then get specific. In other words, we make the story relevant to everybody with a general topic, and then we make it relevant to us by connecting it to our own personal story. For example: Say you have a funny story like mine about being in China (statistically a lot more probable if you're Chinese). Few of your listeners are likely to have visited China, so to start the story and grab maximum attention, make it more relatable. For example, "Sometimes being in a new place can be challenging" is relatable to many, whereas "I was in China last year" is specific to you. Many people will never have traveled overseas, many will never have been to China, but all will have been in a new place at some stage in their lives. Invite the audience into your story. Give them something they can relate to. Remember, the most powerful thing you can do with story is to allow the audience to see themselves within it.

> "Invite the audience into your story. Give them something they can relate to. Remember, the most powerful thing you can do with story is to allow the audience to see themselves within it."

Once you have identified a personal story that connects to your general topic, it's time to start cutting out words. Now you can get to the details—in comedy the funny part is always in the details. Identify the story's key details and trim out unnecessary information that gets in their way. We want to narrow the story down as much as we can to draw out the funny. Keep the following rule of thumb in mind when you are telling a story in front of an audience and building toward a punch line: a three-line span with nothing funny said is too much.

The point is to not drag the story out on your way to the funny part the way, say, my aunt does:

> I went up to visit Mary, and she was fine. It was a warm day. I like warm days. They are much better than cold days. Do you remember that really cold day last year? It was freezing. I had to wear two jackets. One was the pink one. And I couldn't find my gloves. I like gloves. [Ten minutes later:] And then I found Mary, she was drunk out of her mind singing Madonna's "Like a Virgin" to a cow!

When my aunt tells me one of her stories, I don't usually realize that I've nodded off until I snore audibly and that startles me awake. ". . . Wait, what? . . . Me? Drunk singing to a cow?"

Entertaining or not, speakers who find themselves muddied in the details likely have lost their audience by the time they get to the funny part. Just like my aunt does. Take too long to introduce a laugh or reach the point of your story, and you'll probably find your laugh lines get met with a few chuckles or, worse yet, snores in a sea of smartphone screens.

We need to identify the key funny parts in our stories and get there as quickly and effectively as possible. We can do this without losing the story format by using the joke structure, which will allow us to deliver the same story in its shortest, most effective form. Let's look at my aunt's example.

> Take too long to introduce a laugh or reach the point of your story and you'll probably find your laugh lines get met with a few chuckles or, worse yet, snores, in a sea of smartphone screens.

Once we identify the key funny part—my aunt finding Mary drunkenly singing to a cow (hopefully not a regular pastime for Mary's sake)—we need to get there as quickly as possible. Stand-up comedians, top TED speakers, and even presidents tend to follow the same joke format for this: (1) setup, (2) punch line, and then (3) taglines.

The **setup** establishes the premise of the joke by providing the audience with the necessary background information. It should use as few words as possible.

The **punch line** is essentially the laugh line. The setup leads the audience in one direction and the punch line surprises them by suddenly going off in a different direction. That twist, that element of surprise, is a punch line's chief ingredient.

Taglines are optional. They are essentially additional punch lines delivered after the initial punch line. Sometimes they build on the original joke and sometimes they add a twist and a surprising new direction.

"Brevity is the soul of wit."
—William Shakespeare

Remember: Always keep the punch line in mind.

Beginning with the setup, determine which details are essential for introducing your story. If it doesn't directly set up your punch line, cut it. In my aunt's story, the only relevant introductory information is, "I went up to visit Mary, and she was fine." Be ruthless as you edit. Treat it like an irrelevant-detail fire sale; every worthless piece of information must go!

In March 2014, AJ Jacobs gave a TED talk on his use of genealogy websites and the unexpected links that make us all, however distantly, related. He is the author of four *New York Times* bestsellers that combine memoir, science, and humor. His talks are always funny and engaging, and examples like the following, highlighting this joke structure and ruthless editing, can be found throughout:

Setup: On researching family genealogy: "It's not all good news. I found a link to Jeffrey Dahmer, the serial killer."

Punch line: "But I will say that that's on my wife's side."

Tagline: "So . . . I want to make that clear. Sorry, honey."

Joke structure is the key to getting to the funny as quickly as possible. The root of every good joke really is the surprise element, the punch line. And the punch line often releases an intentionally built-up tension.

A great example of this tension comes from the book *Good to Great* by Jim Collins. In this book, Jim details a speech delivered by the ex-CEO of Kimberly-Clark, Darwin Smith, a man described by CNN as one of the ten greatest company leaders of all time. Smith stood up and commenced his talk by saying, "Okay. I want everybody to rise and give a moment of silence." Everybody looked around confused, wondering who had died. They looked down uncomfortably and stared at their shoes in silence. Darwin allowed this process to continue for a period of time. Then he looked down at the group and said in the somber tone, "That was a moment of silence for Procter & Gamble." The place went bananas. At the time, Procter & Gamble was Kimberly-Clark's biggest competitor. Intentionally building up the tension created the laughter that followed, which was essentially a nervous release of energy.

The punch line shatters the intentionally built-up interest and expectation. According to corporate humorist John Kinde, "A funny line is sometimes said to be like a train wreck. You know where the train (your train of thought) has been, you think you know where it's going, but then you're surprised when it goes off track."[21]

As outlined by Mel Helitzer and Mark Shartz in their best-selling book, *Comedy Writing Secrets*, this can be summarized as:

P = Preparation (the situation setup)
A = Anticipation (this can be often achieved with just a timely pause)
P = Punch line (story/joke payoff)

The importance of holding the surprise phrasing to the last possible moment cannot be overemphasized.

London-born Matt Kirshen's precision wit has earned him an impressive reputation on the international comedy circuit with accompanying appearances on *Late Night with Jimmy Fallon*,

The Late Late Show with Craig Ferguson, and a spot as finalist on NBC's *Last Comic Standing*. His best bit of comedic advice to business speakers: Put the word the joke hinges on at the end of the sentence. For example, if the fact it's a cat is the surprise or twist, don't say, "There was a cat in the box." Say, "In that box was a cat." That way you're not still talking when then audience is meant to be laughing.

When President Obama stood before Congress in 2011, he gave his "favorite example" of how messy the government can be (the setup/introduction). "The Interior Department is in charge of salmon while they're in fresh water, but the Commerce Department handles them when they're in saltwater," Obama said. "I hear it gets even more complicated once they're smoked."[22] Not exactly viral hilarity by stand-up comedy standards, but it certainly was in comparison to the usual speeches given in Congress. Placing the impact word at the end of the sentence is not just important for comedic effect; it applies to all key points. If your company wants to highlight its year-on-year growth figure of 80 percent, then you should go out of your way to put this metric at the end of the sentence. Not "We had 80 percent growth year on year," but "We had a year-on-year growth rate of 80 percent."

At the time of writing, creativity expert Ken Robinson has the most viewed talk on TED with more than thirty-six million views. His talk challenges the way we're educating our children and champions a radical rethink of our school systems by cultivating creativity and acknowledging multiple types of intelligence. Make no doubt about it, it is a serious topic, but its masterful delivery is laced with humorous stories and anecdotes. Here is an example of one of them.

We moved from Stratford to Los Angeles, and I just want to say a word about the transition. My son didn't want to come; I've got two kids, he's twenty-one now, and my daughter is sixteen. He didn't want to come to Los Angeles. He loved it, but he had a girlfriend in England. This was the love of his life. Sarah. He'd known her for a month. Mind you, they'd had their fourth anniversary, because it's a long time when you are sixteen. He was really upset on the plane. He said, "I'll never find another girl like Sarah." And we were rather pleased about that, frankly. Because she was the main reason we were leaving the country.

This is a great, funny short story. The only thing a comedian may do is flip the intro with the aim of making it as relevant to everyone as possible before getting more specific (e.g., "Moving to a new place can be challenging. We moved from Stratford to LA"), then cue the rest of the story.

The daunting feeling that comes with arriving in a new place can be a very common one. It's a feeling I know all too well. I went to China for the first time a few years ago. I was worried because the colleague who was looking after me there had previously come to visit me in San Francisco and endured quite a shock. A very conservative man, he asked me, "David, could you recommend activity most enjoyable for Chinese man in San Francisco?" I sent him to the Folsom Street Fair (the world's biggest leather and fetish event). Not quite what he had in mind. When I went to China, he went out of his way to repay the joke.

This is my story from The Moth storytelling competition in short form. The first laugh line is, "I sent him to the Folsom Street Fair." I know where this laugh line is from telling it to friends and colleagues alike, and I suspect it is the same with Ken's TED talk. Knowing where the laugh will likely come improves your timing and delivery. You know when to pause to allow the audience to laugh. In my story, it's a twist in their expectations while their mind scans through traditional tourist activities they would expect to recommend to a conservative visitor. The laugh occurs because we derail their expectations, and this causes a shock to their thoughts. This is the essence of joke structure.

> "As a creator, it's your job to make an audience as excited and fascinated about a subject as you are, and real life tends to do that."
> **—Ricky Gervais**

There's always a funny or a humorous relatable element in real-life stories. The key is to tie them to your overall macro concept and get to laugh lines as quickly and effectively as possible. Keep it relevant to everybody on a macro level before going micro and adding detail. Start general, and then go to something more specific. To build a store of these humorous elements, aim to write ten new jokes a week. This sounds like a lot to start with, but as you begin to take notes and observe the world around you while looking for humor, you'll have plenty of opportunities to find it. Every time you think of something funny or you have an observation or something that you think will be useful, make sure you write it down. If you have a smartphone, use your notes section or an app like Evernote. Otherwise, use a small pad and a pen. You'll be surprised just how quickly you forget these thoughts, so make sure you keep track of them. You want to build a file of jokes that you can draw from and make relevant to every topic on which you're going to present.

> There's always a funny or a humorous relatable element in real-life stories. The key is to tie them to your overall macro concept and get to laugh lines as quickly and effectively as possible. Keep it relevant to everybody on a macro level before going micro and adding detail.

The following example was used consistently by a top business executive and can be found online. It's an early version of a talk that became more polished as it was given more often and had a big impact on the speaker's career. It contains a good humorous example, and by using it, he has become known as a funny and popular speaker. In written form, it's painful to read, but it highlights just how many unnecessary filler words are in there.

Setup:

"You know like, as Global VP for Unilever, I end up traveling a hell of a lot, you know like, I'm based in London but travel to the US every six weeks or so, and eh, it can be kind of tedious at times, like, going to always like the same place but one of the things I really enjoy are kind of like the conversations, that happen along the way, eh, and I must say that coming to JFK I always have like a story to tell about the customs, eh, officer, eh when I hand over my blue Brazilian passport, eh, it's always like, eh, a fun story. And there was one that happened I think, it was like April, May this year. People who follow me on Twitter, Facebook, I even posted that back then.

Main part of story:

"So I arrived there, eh, gave my passport, got the classic. 'So what brings you here?'... And I said 'Work.' I come here a lot for work. And then the guy said and, 'What do you do?' and I said, 'Eh, I work in Marketing at Unilever.' And he said, 'Uni what?' and I said, 'I work for Dove.' And then he said, 'Marketing?' And I said yes. And then he asked something that really surprised me. He asked me, 'But why does Dove need marketing? Everyone knows Dove.' Seriously, he did really say that."

Laugh line:

"And eh, I laughed at first, it was kind of like a nervous laugh because I was afraid I was going to lose my job like . . . right there . . . (audience laugh here) . . . for the guy, arriving in JFK."

He knows the laugh line well, as he has delivered the talk before. His downfall is in the excessive words he uses to get to it. Over time, he has shortened the number of words it takes to get to the laugh line, but this process, like that encountered by most business speakers and those presenting infrequently, took him too long to realize. It happens all too often by trial and error. We want to make it a strategic process.

Now let's rework this example using comedy writing techniques:

Setup:

Relevant to everyone:
Work often leads to business travel.
Specific to him:
Because I have a Brazilian passport, immigration always produces some interesting interactions.

Main part of story:

Last time the conversation went like this:
   What brings you here? (Ideally use a different voice for the officer to differentiate the characters.)
   I come here a lot for work.
   What do you do?
   I work in Marketing at Unilever.
   Uni what?
   I work for Dove.
   Marketing?
   Yes
   Does Dove need marketing? Everybody knows Dove.

Laugh line

I laughed, but it was a nervous laugh as I thought I was going to, right then and there, lose my job. (End on the laugh line. Allow the audience time to laugh. The only additional words should be extra jokes/taglines.)
   Introduction: 138 vs. 18 words.
   Main part of story: 95 vs. 43 words.
   It took our speaker about ninety seconds to get to the funny, when it could have taken approximately forty or less. In a world where you are competing with hyperconnectivity, ever-decreasing attention spans, and shrinking time slots, this is a lot of extraneous time. Don't get me wrong—I like him a lot as a presenter (as do the audiences). I recognize that he is not a native English speaker, and I am amazed by his talk overall. But it could be funnier and more efficient using techniques that comedians know only too well. Get to the laugh lines as quickly as you can and cut out all the unnecessary words along the way.

The main takeaways from this section are that we need to take our stories, work to extract the main funny item, and feed that into a joke structure. This is going to be a process we're going to repeat over and over again as we prepare to build humor items into our presentations and speaking.

Ask yourself: What is the funny twist or part of your story, and how can you get there as quickly as possible without getting lost in unnecessary elements? If this story involves the police force of Hampton Beach, New Hampshire, my advice would be to open the door.

Exercise: Identify the Funny and Link Stories to Topics

Go back to your list from chapter one, take your favorite stories, and write about them for ten minutes. Don't stop to add structure; just let the words flow as much as possible. It can be a life lesson, a cool product, things that drive you crazy, insightful information from a book you are reading, whatever. Don't focus too much on the content at this point; this is simply a writing exercise.

Here we want to identify what you like best, are already comfortable talking about, and are excited to tell people. We also want to find hidden details your mind might have temporarily misplaced.

Now work to find the key point to each story. Where is the funny anecdote, interesting bit of knowledge, or the entertaining part? Work to cut out unnecessary words and retell the best stories following the joke structure (i.e., setup, punch line, and taglines if you have any). Don't worry if you can't come up with anything immediately. Often this process can take a few days or even weeks. The important thing is that you begin to think about your list of stories. Most of my best ones come to me when I am out and about—letting my subconscious do the work—rather than when I am sitting at a desk.

Start to think about your stories as they connect to general topics and make a list of what areas they could be included under. Remember, the connection can be quite loose and rely on the right introduction (setup) or takeaway to make it work well in a business content that initially seems unlikely.

For example, my list, which for weeks initially had nothing at all, began to look like this:

Funny File

1. **Technology/New Users:** My Dad sending me long emails all in the subject line.
2. **Market Entry (know your competitive landscape or you may learn a painful lesson):** As a child, urinating by accident on an electrical fence.
3. **Maslow's Hierarchy of Needs/Compensation:** Getting a job offer from a startup that told me they had no budget for me but could "buy me a few nice meals."
4. **Social Media:** Facebook post contrasting US positivity with Irish outlook. US comment: "Kitesurfing under the Golden Gate Bridge, that looks amazing, you are so lucky." Irish comment: "I hope a shark bites your balls off."
5. **Experience-Based Learning:** Using the Spanish word for female private parts in place of "Bless you" with a Guatemalan host family for two whole months. To make it worse the father was a local preacher.
6. **Proper Planning:** While working on a whale shark research boat in Honduras, instructing a group of snorkelers to swim with a whale shark that turned out to be a tiger shark (with a lot more teeth!).
7. **Cost Cutting/Budgeting:** As a student being paid to mow lawns with no grass in Nantucket.
8. **Confidence:** New Year's Eve in Salvador, Brazil, I ended up drinking one too many vodka coconuts (very manly I know) and recorded a TV interview live from the beach for Brazil's main TV station . . . in Portuguese. I didn't speak much Portuguese at the time. I did, it seems, after vodka coconuts.
9. **Getting Out of the Comfort Zone:** My Australian friend, Matt, calling me when he arrived in Bogotá,

Colombia, with no Spanish and telling me he was on "Calle Street" (*calle* in Spanish means "street").

10. **Health/Sports/Customer Service:** Breaking my ankle in Greece and, in place of a doctor, getting a vet.

11. **Statistics:** Ireland has more Nobel Prizes than China. A true superpower?

12. **Unnecessary Conversations:** Guy at my local supermarket who asks me daily, "Did you find everything okay?" Of course I did. It's a supermarket and I came here looking for food . . . what did you expect to happen?

13. **Habit:** My mother finding me drunkenly calling my cat's name out the back garden. He was dead four years at the time. Something I had forgotten.

14. **Asking the Right Questions:** Homeless man asking me if I had a spare sandwich.

15. **Innovation (needed!):** Frustration of calling American automated customer service lines with an Irish accent.

16. **Expectations/Operations:** Rushing my mother to the accident and emergency ward in the hospital when she broke her hip, only to be informed the ward was closed.

17. **False Advertising/Marketing:** Philippines-based rebel group that doesn't sound too bad to many American males: Moro Islamic Liberation Front or MILF for short.

18. **Recruitment:** Transport company Uber advertising for people within its corporate division with "the fear tolerance of a honey badger." What do they plan on doing to employees?

19. **Dyslexia/Embarrassment/Mistakes:** Ending spinal cord injury fundraising emails in error with "Kind retards, Davdi." Had to be pointed out to me by friends. Sometimes I tried to be office cool, dropped

the kind part, and just signed off with "Retards." Not good. Not good at all.

20. **Leadership/HR Issues/Quotes Not to Live By:** My old boss's favorite expression at a summer job moving furniture: "The hands will heal, boys, but the furniture won't." He was wrong. Piano 1, David 0. My revenge came when I accidently dropped a large steel-loading ramp through the side of his truck. Rather than admitting to the twelve-inch hole it left, I used Scotch tape to cover it up and wrote on it the words, "This is not a hole."

21. **Innovation/Productivity Hacks/Strategy:** Guy at the park who sat on the wall drinking beer while casting a ball to his dog via a fishing rod he had attached it to.

22. **Talking to Customers/Feedback:** Waiter at a local restaurant who greets me, and everyone else by saying, all in one sentence, "How are you today I am fine thanks for asking." Giving no opportunity to respond, whatsoever.

23. **Management Relations:** My old boss Roberts Diane (I have spelled her name backwards to protect her identity) disliked me so much, she spent money to have me edited out of a team photo with the then Irish president that hung proudly above her desk.

24. **Family and Work (very likely connected to number 23):** I was responsible for the invitation list for a reception with the Irish president held at Microsoft's headquarters. I of course added everyone I knew in the area, family included. Which was fine until the president's speech made one very large man in the audience so emotional that he rushed the stage, amid frantic secret service agents, to hug the President. That man was my uncle . . . Not ideal.

25. **Career Transition:** The former rap star MC Hammer is now an active startup company angel investor. He must be a pain to have around the office. He would never let you touch anything.

26. **The Sales Process:** Young girl who approached me on the beach in Cambodia: "You wan hair removal?"

    Eh, no, thanks.

    "Why no, you hairy like monkey. You no buy from me I kill you like fruit salad."

It's important to add here that my stories as listed from travel overseas can get good laughs, but those that get the best reactions are the ones that come from everyday occurrences, like that time in the supermarket. Few folks, thankfully, have thrown unsuspecting tourists into the ocean to swim in error with tiger sharks. Nearly everyone, however, has been to the supermarket. More often than not, relatability wins.

Can I link the above examples to business presentations? I most certainly can, and so can you with yours. Are they more engaging and entertaining than widget examples? Most certainly. If you take nothing else from this book, please do stop defaulting to widget examples (unless you make them). Have you ever been excited to hear a presenter's wild, entertaining, and fictional widget example? One would certainly hope not.

#3 Write Funny

"A sense of humor is an attitude in how you approach your work and life. It is a skill that can be developed."
—Jeanne Robertson

Ryan is a socially awkward guy. He is long and narrow, walks lazily with the grace of a drunken penguin, and speaks with a hint of insanity. He doesn't maintain eye contact, looks disheveled, and comes across as a bag of nerves. He has a comb-over about twenty years premature and rides a skateboard that makes him look about twenty years immature. He is shy and struggles to converse with anyone. It was hard to believe he was about to take the stage as a comedian.

I met Ryan in the little-known intellectual capital of California, a small city called Stockton. I was there for another comedy show. In most places, when I start to speak with my Irish accent, I'm met with the same question: Where in Ireland are you from? In most dumb places, I hear, "Where is Ireland?" Not in Stockton. In Stockton, I was asked, *What is Ireland?* A rich source of material at least.

Ryan was to this point the least funny person I had met. But when his time came to go on stage, he suddenly looked quietly confident. He abandoned the skateboard and suddenly gained a spring in his step. His eyes, previously easily distracted, were now laser-focused on the microphone and the eagerly awaiting crowd baying for entertainment. The stage rose five feet above the audience, but he moved with such intention that he made the steep steps to reach it seem like they weren't even there.

He took the microphone in one hand and used his other to move the supporting stand to one side, removing the only obstacle that stood between him and the audience. He stood with a newfound poise and confidence before a packed house and took a moment to survey those about to judge him. The guy whom I would have bet my house on not being funny was about to prove me wrong. *Very wrong.*

Ryan wasted no time whipping the audience into a frenzy of loud, often uncontrollable laughter, and he kept this going for a full ten minutes. He put the microphone back in the stand after delivering his last, best joke to huge applause and appreciation as the room pulsated with a new energy. He exited the stage like a king and quickly went back to being really unfunny. The laser-focused eyes returned to easy distractions, but he now had a spring in his step and a wry smile on his face. What he just did felt really good. Like a baseball player hitting a home run with the bases loaded or a soccer player scoring a winning goal in a final, Ryan had just done what he had trained to do and had done it to perfection.

Then he did his best to ruin the moment by vomiting into a garbage can, snorting up a piece of pizza, and exiting the building Tony Hawk–style without another word. What just happened?

Very few comedians I met over the last year were what I would describe as naturally funny. Many were in fact the complete opposite, like Ryan. The natural gifts weren't there but the skill certainly was—and it was clear that they developed their skill through practice, particularly in writing. Over time, these unfunny people learned how to write better and better.

> "Good writing helps good marketers become great marketers. If you have a website, you are a publisher. If you are on social media, you are in marketing. And that means we are all writers. Our writing can make us look smart or it can make us look stupid. It can make us seem fun, or warm, or competent, or trustworthy—or it can make us seem humdrum or discombobulated or flat-out boring."
> **–Ann Handley**

Don't get me wrong. Some comedians are naturally hilarious people. They seem to have an innate talent for being funny. From what I have seen over the last year, these comedians tend to rise to the top of their industry quicker than those who just rely on writing alone. We are not trying to be comedians, however. We are trying to become funnier speakers, and what we learn from those who are not naturally funny will do just fine.

Everyone knows that comedy is essentially a combination of what you say and how you say it—your material and your delivery. The often-unmentioned third element is how you write it. The same can be said for public speaking. Every great presentation, like every great joke, is first crafted with a pen, pencil, or keyboard. Mastering the skill of writing, therefore, will improve your public speaking ability no matter how naturally ungifted you are.

Good comedians are good writers, too. As their writing gets better, they get funnier. Few admit it, but they all demonstrate that a sense of humor can be developed and further refined with practice. Practicing your delivery is important, of course, but by learning the skills that go with good comedy writing, you can be funnier more quickly and ultimately a better and more entertaining public speaker.

In this chapter, we're going to go through a number of ways that you can quickly and effectively bring additional humor elements to your presentation using comedy-writing techniques. These techniques are often widely used by copywriters and learned the hard way by aspiring comedians. All are utilized by great public speakers.

Work in references to the local area where possible.

On a very hot summer's day in 1962, President John F. Kennedy visited Rice University in Houston, Texas, and gave a speech in the football stadium. One of his more famous quotes from that day is a joke mocking the university's football team: "But why, some say, the moon? Why choose this as our goal? And they may well ask why climb the highest mountain? Why, thirty-five years ago, fly the Atlantic? Why does Rice play Texas?"[23]

The University of Texas was undefeated and Rice University was winless at that point in the year. The line got a huge laugh.

By adding a local reference, like JFK did, you're showing the attendees at your conference or presentation that you have an understanding of that area. The majority of people in attendance at any presentation or seminar will likely be from that local catchment area. (Disclaimer: There are exceptions to this rule. Please don't contact me saying you gave a presentation in Albuquerque to the Japanese Albuquerque United Consumer Association and your sushi line fell on deaf ears. Know your audience. This is a rule of thumb—and sometimes rules of thumb are as effective as a blind, drunk, one-winged homing pigeon.) By working in local references—whether it's simply referencing certain affluent areas, calling on local sporting rivalries, or recognizing challenges or issues pertaining to specific parts of town—you demonstrate that you have a special understanding and interest in their location. When I talk to an audience in San Francisco about the collective intellect of Stockton, it's a joke specifically for them and they know it. This is a chance to add really quick and easy jokes and win over the crowd.

Make sure you set the scene.

Every good comedian makes sure he or she sets set up a joke by painting a picture so the audience can relate to the experience. A great piece of advice given to me by one of the San Francisco Bay Area's top comedians, Reggie Steele, is to write as if you are describing something to a blind person. It's a piece of advice he learned literally when a number of blind people came to one of his shows. He wanted to make sure they could relate to his story and follow every aspect of it from the words alone and not just his usual animated style.

Add attitude to your writing and presentations.

You want to use words like *weird, amazing, scary, hard, stupid, crazy,* or *nuts.* Try to incorporate these words into your opening setup or statement. I tested the following example of this with a joke at Cobb's Comedy Club, San Francisco: *It's crazy how soft modern-day workers have become. Imagine them one hundred years ago on an expedition to the Antarctic with*

Ernest Shackleton and the great explorers of old. Captain's log: "Only ten days into the journey and we have had to abandon the voyage, due to the tragic loss of the lives of sixty-two of the men, to what has be described as . . . a gluten allergy." Behind these lines are my own struggles as an expatriate business manager getting used to differing work practices and culture in San Francisco. The use of an attitude word (*crazy*) in the setup helps people focus and pay attention quickly. If you want people to be passionate about your topic, show them some passion.

Make sure you give clear takeaways.

When you're crafting a story or a joke, you want to leave people with something to remember. In our presentations, we'll do exactly the same thing. When you see "1,000 songs in your pocket," you'll immediately think about Steve Jobs and the launch of the iPod. This was the key takeaway, 1,000 songs in your pocket. He repeated it over and over throughout the presentation. Also, Martin Luther King, Jr. repeated, "I have a dream," the key line from his famous speech, to emphasize it as the clear takeaway.

The third most popular TED talk at the time of writing is Simon Sinek's "How Great Leaders Inspire Action." He repeatedly states the main point of the talk: "People don't buy what you do, they buy why you do it." Chris Rock is also known for doing this. He will emphasize exactly what he wants you to take away from the joke continually throughout the performance, making sure it's firmly planted in your mind.

Use callbacks.

Callbacks bring everything together in the end. This is where you go back (call back) and reference items that have had a good reaction or response from the crowd. This can be one of your jokes that worked or a joke from a previous presenter that got a big laugh. Callbacks are a great technique for linking your topic together and really build the audience into an in-joke between you and them. The callback works best if you have moved on to another topic before using it, to create an element of surprise. In JFK's example, a callback would involve referencing his initial Rice/Texas joke again later in his presentation.

Chris Guillebeau is a best-selling nonfiction author who visited every country in the world over a ten-year period. Chris has been known to tour more than fifty cities to promote the release of a new book. He's a really great presenter and always includes humor in his speaking engagements.

While answering a question from an audience member who looked very youthful, Chris asked, "How old are you, fourteen?"

"Twenty-two," the kid responded.

"Oops."

Everyone laughed.

At the close of his talk Chris directed the gathered audience to seek advice not just from him, but also fellow travelers in the room, including "the fourteen-year-old." Another laugh. This was a classic callback and reference to a joke between Chris and the audience that already worked.

Callbacks are rarely funny to read but always effective in the moment, as they are all about a shared experience between the audience and the speaker. As a rule of thumb, don't call back to a joke more than three times, and definitely don't call back to something that wasn't funny in the first place.

Use current media references where possible.

Creating material that relates to topics that are current in the mind of those in our audience is another easy way to get a laugh. Nighttime television hosts like John Oliver, Stephen Colbert, and Jimmy Fallon are masters of this, and their popularity heightens the chance that your crowd already will be familiar with poking fun at fresh topics. Celebrities, politicians, and sporting teams are normally easy and acceptable targets. This also gives the illusion of spontaneity due to the short-preparation time scale if something just happened. Don't go overboard, though. Keep media references to less than 10 percent of your total content. Also, be sensible here. If a plane just crashed, taking 100 souls with it, this is not the time to reference it.

Incorporate act-outs or use of different voices where possible.

Conversational interaction between two characters gives us the chance to bring the scene to life on stage and puts the audience directly into the action. If you can do different voices or different accents or speak another language, it's a great way to incorporate your skills and show them off while writing them into your stories. Even taking an accent your ears are very accustomed to, like your partner's or parents', will work better than just playing both characters in your own voice. But be mindful of how you sound. It's always safer to change your voice slightly rather than take on a whole new nationality. Be careful to stay away from impersonations that may be seen as politically incorrect. I have been subject to way too many dodgy Irish impersonations in my life, and the same can be said for many other groups. Unless you are really, really good at it, keep it simple. As a guiding principle, think family members before foreigners!

Don't create these act-outs on paper. Make sure you say them aloud and record how you sound. Then review your recording, take notes, and refine your writing.

Always write in the present tense.

You never want to write, "I was walking and I saw." It should be, "I'm walking and I see." Even if the event happened many, many years ago, you want the audience to be living that moment with you as if it's happening right now. Write the scene for the audience as if it's unfolding in front of their very eyes. Again, your writing will be much more engaging if the audience feels like they're a part of the action.

Use inherently funny words.

Believe it or not, some words are funnier than others and can be amusing without any given context. In an interview with the *New York Times,* Jerry Seinfeld talked about how he wrote his bit about Pop-Tarts. He took foods from the sixties in all their strange, frozen, unhealthy forms and narrowed his focus on Pop-Tarts. Why Pop-Tarts? Because *Pop-Tarts* sounds funny: "The Pop-Tart suddenly appeared in the supermarket . . . and we were like chimps in the dirt playing with sticks." According to Seinfeld, what makes the joke, "is you have got chimps, dirt, playing, and sticks. In seven words, four of them are funny. Chimps, chimps are funny." In one *Seinfeld* episode, "The Apology," Jerry has a naked lady wanting to snack on pickles. Why pickles? Because pickles are funny.

In *The Sunshine Boys*, Neil Simon quips, "Words with a 'K' in it are funny. Alka-Seltzer is funny. Chicken is funny. All with a 'K.' L's are not funny. M's are not funny." *Simpsons* creator Matt Groening proclaimed the word *underpants* to be at least 15 percent funnier than the word *underwear*.[24] *Pants* are funny. The name of one of Groening's characters, Krusty the Clown, was, like many others, not created by chance. Words with "K" sounds are just funnier. Comedians and comedy writers know this and use these funny-sounding words consciously. So should you.

Remember, "brevity is levity."

We want to get to the funny or punch line as quickly as possible. Copywriter Henneke Duistermaat lists some great words to watch out for that can usually be cut out: *ought, in my opinion, that, just, actually, truly,* and *very.* These are all words that can be stripped out to get to the punch line quicker. Watch out for them in your writing. Scott Adams, the creator of the comic strip *Dilbert,* notes, "Keep your writing simple, as if you were sending a witty email to a friend. Be smart, but not academic. Prune words that don't make a difference."[25]

Use the Rule of 3.

According to Greek philosopher and mathematician Pythagoras, three, which he called "triad," is the noblest of all digits. The number three has held sway over math, science, astronomy, arts, and literature for millennia until, finally, it reached its apex in 1973 with the pilot episode of *Schoolhouse Rock!* As the episode's theme song notes, we have "the past and the present and the future" and "the heart and the brain and the body" among many trios.

Not quite Greek philosophy, but the number three's magic is widely known and used by writers, marketers, and comedians alike. If you want to write in a more entertaining and memorable manner, write with the Rule of 3. This rule is a basic structure for jokes and ideas that capitalizes on the way we process information. By necessity, we have become proficient at pattern recognition. Three is the smallest number of elements required to create a pattern. This combination of pattern and brevity results in memorable content. And that's why the Rule of 3 will make you a more engaging writer.

This rule has existed for a long time, but I had to figure it out through trial and error. When I told jokes in certain sequences, I noticed they were always most effective when I reworked them into groups of three. It seemed that audiences were trained to laugh on the third item. So, if I made one quick joke and a second quick joke, the laugh would always be biggest on the third one. If I remove any of these elements (leaving only two) or added extra ones (creating four or five), the bit is never as effective. It's strange, but true.

At its most basic, the Rule of 3 establishes a pattern then ends with something unexpected. This derailment, a break away from the pattern created by the first two items, builds tension, and creates surprise usually resulting in loud laughter.

Information presented in groups of three also sticks in our head better than other clusters of items. For example: "life, liberty, and the pursuit of happiness," "blood, sweat, and tears," "sex, lies, and videotape." When the iPhone was launched, it was launched as three products (iPod, phone, Internet communicator device) all in one new cool product. It was no coincidence that it was pitched in this way. It automatically became more memorable. Examples are seemingly endless: NFL, NBA, NHL, CNN, NBC, BBC, UPS, SAS, SAP, "Just do it," "Yes we can"—get the idea?

Jokes Using the Rule of 3

Let's have a look at the Rule of 3 in action with a couple of jokes. Written out and analyzed like this they don't sound that exciting, but when delivered to a live audience, they generate big laughs.

The first one comes from Jon Stewart:

"I celebrated Thanksgiving in an old-fashioned way. I invited everybody in my neighborhood to my house, we had an enormous feast, and then I killed them and took their land."

The twist here is obviously the last part. The triplet in the set, "I killed them and took their land," comes as a shock because he used the first two parts of the joke to create an event in your mind that is very familiar; this way, you think you know where you're going to end up. He starts with a broad picture and something everyone will understand: "Thanksgiving in an old-fashioned way." Then he begins to narrow the vision in a way that his audience will relate to and personalize: "I invited everyone in the neighborhood, we had an enormous feast." These lines allow you to recreate your own Thanksgiving memories in your mind, thus making you feel like you know where he's heading. Then, the twist, the derailment, the laugh line, always third in the set: "and then I killed them and took their land."

This next joke is one I wrote when I was starting out in comedy. I wrote it when I learned of this pattern. To be honest, I hate telling it, but it follows the structure and sequence, uses the Rule of 3, and always produces a big laugh every time:

"My girlfriend is always driving me crazy about going to Napa. I gave in and brought her. It turns out she doesn't even like auto parts."

With the first two parts of this joke I am creating the image of California's wine country, conjuring up images of couples spending time drinking wine in this famous region. NAPA, of course, with uppercase letters, is also a chain of automotive service centers—the last place in the world my girlfriend would want to go.

That is the third item in the sequence. That is where the pattern breaks. Due to this twist, the punch line, this joke gets a big laugh every time I'm on stage. By following the Rule of

3, whether it is in your joke writing or even just in the way you deliver important information, your words are far more likely to be memorable. Your audience's minds are ready to receive information in groups of three. You should use that to your advantage.

Use funny images and video.

While you should prioritize the time to write some humor into your presentations, sometimes that's easier said than done. If you feel too busy to step back for a moment and look at simple ways to add some creativity that, in our case, is aimed at generating laughs and lightening the mood, then you can rely on funny images and video to do that for you. The following image was used to great laughter in a TED talk to make the point: "Entrepreneurs: We are the rule breakers."

"Presentations have an extra advantage over most traditional stand-up comedy sets—a giant friggin' screen that the audience is staring at the whole time you're onstage," says Sammy Wegent, long-time comedian and creator of the improv PowerPoint comedy show Speechless Live. "In a world where funny Photoshopped images, memes, and GIFs dominate our devices, visual humor has never been bigger. So don't just say funny things in your presentation. Show funny things, too," he advises.

It's great if these images or videos are your own, but they do not have to be. Go on Google Images and type "funny" and then your topic area. More often than not you will come up with a usable image that most of your audience will not have seen before. The key is tying this image to your topic and using it to reinforce a point. Image archive sites like Reddit, Imgur, and Pinterest are another great source of content that is already socially proven. Often you just need to change one word or the setup, or overlay some text, to integrate it into your speech.

My friend Jill had to give a high-level talk recently at a conference organized by LinkedIn, and she wanted to add some humor points to increase engagement. Rather than using words alone to describe how she was feeling in her job when they were experiencing a period of hypergrowth, she showed an image of what she felt like. "Right here . . . I look very calm and collected and happy," she said, showing a picture of her at her desk with her colleagues. "When in reality how I remember that time is more like this," she added before revealing another image of a small girl being blasted in the face by an out-of-control water hose. The audience broke out in laughter.

Seth Godin, the writer and marketer I mentioned in chapter one, is also known for his engaging and entertaining presentations. His talk titled "This Is Broken" is always referred to, even by TED itself, as hilarious. And it is. To put it into perspective, he makes people laugh approximately 3.4 times per minute through his twenty-minute talk. If you apply the same loose metric (more on this in chapter seven) to Hollywood's top comedy movies, he actually makes people laugh more times than such comedy classics as *Airplane!*, *The Hangover,* and *The Naked Gun.* As presenters go, Seth is excellent and always funny. However, when we analyze his talks, we realize they are considerably funnier the more funny images he includes. In this talk, over half of the laughs stem from jokes linked to images he included.

Use the same joke structure with images and videos as you would with written material. Set up your image with an introduction that builds anticipation. The image becomes the punch line and should be enough to solicit a laugh, as it was for Jill. Then you have a chance to keep people laughing through taglines (your additional comments on the image or video). Seth and Jill are by no means alone in using images. Keep an eye out for just how many laughs occur in presentations with the use of funny images.

Remember: There is always a more creative way to introduce your idea. If you are worried about clever writing or your delivery, using videos and images can be a great way of taking the pressure off while bringing the laugh levels up. A little effort here can go a long way.

These quick comedy tips, when taken together and added to your presentation, can make a big impact in generating humor every time. They will not make you a funnier person in life, but, like Ryan, they will make you funnier on stage. And if you want to make it especially easy, my advice is to head out to Stockton. It doesn't take much to impress the rocket surgeons out there.

Exercise: Linking Stories to Your Presentation

List what problem your product, service, or research solves on a general (macro) and specific (micro) level. This should be based on the next presentation topic you intend to speak on or your most recently given one. Now aim to link your presentation topic to your life stories, observations, and experiences, as listed previously.

How can you write your story into your presentation? Are there any correlations between your topics and your stories? If you are struggling for links, don't worry. There is always a way to work funny items in. Remember, crafting a funny story involves knowing the ending and working backward. You want to find that funny bit and design your talk to build it in. Ken Robinson's talk did this masterfully, and he is far from alone in doing so.

For example, say your company has a more user-friendly touch screen with bigger characters or buttons. This makes it easier for elderly people and those with vision problems to use. Cue stories about your parents or grandparents trying to use technology.

Macro/wider topic: It makes it easier for elderly people to use technology.

Micro/specific problem my product solves: It makes it easier for elderly people to type and use smart phones/tablets.

Key funny to my story: My dad's struggles with technology and specifically what he does by writing emails in the subject line.

The setup intro here becomes the challenges elderly people have adapting to and using technology, specifically email in my case. This should be delivered in as few words as possible.

This example is far from a classic, but it is a quick and easy joke that gets laughs:

It's sometimes hard for elderly people to get to grips with technology. (Relatable setup)

My Dad (specific to me) *finally tried sending email last year. He wrote me a fine long one . . .*

All in the subject box. (Punch line)

He continues to do this. (Tagline)

Show staged image of my Dad looking confused or socially proven funny image found online.

Following the joke structure and the above example, try and create one joke with the fewest words possible from your favorite story that can be linked to your company/product/service/research. Use the Rule of 3 and as many as these tips as you can.

Search sites like Reddit, Imgur, and Pinterest for socially proven funny images that you can link to your topic. These images can also be your own, but they certainly do not have to be.

Remember: You are not trying to be the next Jerry Seinfeld. A little laughter is better than 90 percent of the business speakers out there.

Rehearsed Spontaneity:
Learning Comedy by Playing Banjo for an Empty Room

> *"Spectacular achievement is always preceded by*
> *unspectacular preparation."*
>
> **—Robert H. Schuller**

When Steve Martin was getting started in comedy, he would do whatever he could simply to get himself on stage. In his autobiography, *Born Standing Up*, he recounts the regular opening-act gig he had at the Coffee and Confusion in San Francisco in 1965. His act at the time consisted of material that he refers to as, "strictly Monday-night quality, the night when, traditionally, anyone could get up to perform."

The Coffee and Confusion was essentially a bare room with some chairs and some lightbulbs, hardly the ideal performance space even on a good day. And on a bad day, the room was 100 percent empty. Even when there wasn't a soul there, Martin had to start his act on time—just in case passersby outside noticed him through the window and were drawn in. "So," he says, "I went on stage and started talking. Talking to no one."

As if that weren't difficult enough, Martin was expected to perform a twenty-five-minute set every night. At the time, he only had about ten minutes of decent comedy material. So he fell back on everything he had: he played banjo, he did magic tricks, he put on costumes and props before settling in to address his audience in a serious manner: "I know what you're thinking, 'Oh, this is just another banjo-magic act.'" If he had an obliging audience, he could make it through the full twenty-five minutes; if not, he'd have to fight not to be dead in the water after twelve. He described it like this: "Afraid of falling short, I ad-libbed, wandered around the audience, talked to patrons, joked with waitresses, and took note of anything unusual that was happening in the crowd and addressed it for laughs, in the hope of keeping my written material in reserve so I could fill my time quota."[26]

As excruciating as that might sound (I know it does to me), it was the ideal practice setting. Steve Martin was getting "stage time, stage time, and stage time" in adverse conditions almost every night. He treated every set like it was important, even if the bouncers were the only other people in the room; he learned what he could fall back on when his audience was tough; and he built a repertoire of fallback jokes and a few in-case-of-emergency jokes. Over time, he was ready for whatever came his way. Years later, he was still using this format—the "unstructured and modern" element of his shows were the defining element of his stand-up career. That success, generally, can be traced back to Comedy Habit #4: Rehearsed Spontaneity.

Ironically, the objective of comedians, as they put almost twenty-two hours of work into every minute of their performance each year, is to make every one of those minutes look spontaneous and effortless. They work to craft a collection of tried and trusted material that flows so well together, in and out between audience interactions, that it appears the comedian just created it all off the top of his or her head in the moment. They are so well practiced by the time it comes to the big event they could do it in the dark. Martin was no different; he took notes after every performance, recording what worked, what didn't, and why.

Billy Connolly is one of my favorite comedians and a storyteller by nature. He tells a six-minute story about an elderly lady taking a bus. When I saw this bit live, it appeared that every bit of the story may have unfolded the day before and Billy just happened to be sharing it with me. Never did it occur to me that every line and word was carefully selected and that every part was a well-rehearsed component.

> The reality is, you can't wing it. If you don't prepare, you may do okay some of the time, poorly all too often, and good occasionally. You have to practice. Practice breeds consistency, good habits, and success. This is something that every comedian, performer, and athlete knows.

The reality is, you can't wing it. If you don't prepare, you may do okay some of the time, poorly all too often, and good occasionally. You have to practice. Practice breeds consistency, good habits, and success. This is something that every comedian, performer, and athlete knows. The work comes prior to the big day, not on the big day. I said at the start of this book that this is not a magic book. Application of these principles won't make you instantly funnier, more successful, or more attractive to the opposite sex. Add a little practice, however, and it just might. It's time for a little practice.

The harder you work, the more natural you will be on stage. Remember the words of world public-speaking champion

Darren LaCroix, "The three keys are stage time, stage time, and stage time." The problem is busy professionals are not able to dedicate time to developing their performance ability every day like aspiring comedians. Don't worry—you don't have to. One practice session every second week combined with some 80/20 Principle tips should be enough to quickly make a big difference. Work presentations count. Every chance you get to talk to somebody . . . anybody . . . counts. Use every chance you can get to speak publicly.

"All things are ready, if our minds be so."
–William Shakespeare, *Henry V*

Practice speaking within shorter and shorter time frames and keep cutting your presentation, speech, or story until someone complains that it's too short. Recognize that modern-day audiences have ever-decreasing attention spans. These short attention spans have led many companies and conferences to shorten their speaking slots as well. Keynotes are becoming TED talks—short, funny, and information packed. Being concise forces you to include only your best points, jokes, and stories. Where there is no time limit, impose one on yourself. Will people complain that your talk should have been longer? Unlikely. And if they do, leaving them wanting more is never a bad thing.

Once you feel comfortable with telling your material and stories to your friends, family, and colleagues, move on to strangers. Don't just run up to people on the street and start your stories—that never ends well. Don't force your opinions on your audience, either; people don't like being told how to think. Keep the focus on telling stories. It will make you so much more likable on stage and, as I've found in my own experience, will make you bomb next to never. The best ways to practice this are via open mics, storytelling nights, and public speaking groups like Toastmasters. If you are short on time, or attending nights like these sounds like a stretch, don't worry. Practicing in any manner, even at home in your underpants to a captive audience like your cat, will still make you better than most speakers out there, who for the most part are winging it. Leave winging it to the birds.

It's worth paying heed to the words of Irish comic Dylan Moran here on relying on your potential alone: "Don't do it! Stay away from your potential. You'll mess it up. It's potential; leave it. Anyway, it's like your bank balance—you always have a lot less than you think."

> Practicing in any manner, even at home in your underpants to a captive audience like your cat, will still make you better than most speakers out there, who for the most part are winging it. Leave winging it to the birds.

This practice should be viewed as a learning experience, as it will highlight areas you need to work on. Your story and humorous bit list will always be in Permanent Beta. Remember, a smile from a colleague, small laugh at an open mic night, or a mild sniffle from your cat often translates to huge laughs at a conference or in a presentation. Business audiences are often so starved of entertainment that by including some in your talk, you can generate reactions in them akin to a group of happy dolphins slapping their hands together loudly as their bodies thrust backward in excited, Flipper-style appreciation. Stage time is at a premium these days and, with more and more professionals crossing the line toward comedy, if you are brave enough to get out there, you'll meet some great and interesting people on these nights. Over the last year I have met TED speakers, startup founders, Emmy-nominated writers, lawyers, sales and software professionals, many great comedians, many terrible comedians, and a huge collection of lunatics all trying to build their public speaking skill set in the same unconventional way.

> "To improve, we must watch ourselves fail, and learn from our mistakes."
> **—Joshua Foer**

Practice as you wish to deliver.

You need to practice your material exactly as you wish to deliver it. If you practice at home in a seated position, it's going to feel strange when you go on stage and have to perform standing.

How you use your hands when you're speaking is extremely important. Don't stand there with your hands in your pockets. You want to engage them as much as you can. In 2015, a human behavior consultancy called Science of People set out to find what makes TED talks go viral. Founder Vanessa Van Edwards identified one of the key nonverbal indicators as hand movements. Her poll revealed a correlation between the number of hand gestures a speaker makes in a talk and the number of views the talk receives.[27]

A great tip given to me by San Francisco–based comedian Matt Morales is to practice your presentation with a bottle in each hand. This gets you accustomed to speaking with your hands out in front of you, which looks really natural but initially will make you feel like a zombie robot.

And whatever you do, don't look at your feet. Focus on something right in front of you as if you're talking to the audience. You want to build the habit of looking ahead with your face up and smiling as you're presenting. These little things can make a big difference in building the right habits. If you want to stand up and talk, don't sit down and practice.

Once you've practiced your material in your home, it's time to get out and test your jokes and stories in the real world. Like Darren LaCroix says: stage time, stage time, stage time. It is the perfect opportunity to identify patterns, jokes, and stories that really hold an audience's attention and hopefully generate some laughs. The best way to do this is in front of live audiences.

Your material and collection of stories are always a work in progress. Record, study, and evaluate each performance continuously. By doing this, you're able to look back and cut out the *ahhhs*, *uhmms*, *ehhhs*, unnecessary words, and gaps in your performance that can be improved (we'll look at this in more detail in chapter five). Record it, realize it, and then cut it out. Identifying these areas helps you create a more polished and effortless-looking talk. You'll also be doing this to find material you know always gets laughs.

Take a bar exam.

If you are not quite ready for live audiences, head for the bar. Unlike conference rooms, bars are friendly, social places. People expect stories told there to be succinct and entertaining. That's why IDEO marketing lead and Mortified co-producer Annette Ferrara tells designers to "take a bar exam"[28]: "Go to a bar with a colleague—or imagine you're in one—and tell your stories using only napkin drawings as your visuals. Have your friend repeat back your story to see what's sticking and what's not. Refine and repeat." I know this wisdom sounds like it has its origins in Irish stereotypes. I would love to deny this, but wholeheartedly I can't. Annette's husband is Irish.

Over-preparation is the best way (if not the only way) to be able to overcome anything that may go haywire during your presentation. Murphy's Law states that what can go wrong will go wrong. Murphy's Law of Public Speaking states that what can go wrong will be ten times worse and go viral. Make sure you have your notes with you and that you're familiar with the concepts. Make sure you have additional copies of your presentation. A great piece of advice is to make sure you're already familiar with the stage and the setup. Try to get on stage before you present. Go during the day, or earlier in the evening, just to stand up there when no one's around and get comfortable with that particular venue.

Video- or audio-record and review every performance. You will be surprised just how much your time on stage can fly by and how little your mind will remember of the experience. We do this to pick up on items we can improve and make sure we catch any bits that worked well. It feels really awkward at first, as most people hate the sound of their own voice. "We hate it because it is so foreign," says Dr. William Cullinan, dean of the College of Health Sciences at Marquette University in Wisconsin.[29] When you hear your own voice you are not hearing it as others do, due to the internal bones and conduits it must pass through to make it to your ears. This is why all of a sudden it seems alien.

Jordan Gaines, a neuroscience grad student at Penn State College of Medicine and a science writer, explains in an *NBC News* article, "It's kind of the same way we like what we see in the mirror, but not what we see in photographs."[30] Many of us will have spent time in front of that very mirror getting ready for a big night out. Happy that we look good and are ready to roll, we leave the house for a great night, and it is great—until the photos get posted on social media the next day. "How did they get one of me that makes me look so ugly?" you think. "It looks nothing like what I saw beforehand in the mirror."

Earlier this year, I was working on writing jokes for a very famous and talented international public figure and speaker. I was amazed to find out he had never once reviewed his own talks. Like the rest of us, he was uncomfortable listening to his own voice and watching himself on screen, but once he tried it a few times, it became habit and his talks quickly got much better and funnier. By recording and reviewing his speaking, he could quickly see the areas he could improve on, and distinguish what jokes were working from those that were not.

> He was uncomfortable listening to his own voice and watching himself on screen, but once he tried it a few times, it became habit and his talks quickly got much better and funnier. By recording and reviewing his speaking, he could quickly see the areas he could improve on, and distinguish what jokes were working from those that were not.

Based on just my gut feeling, I thought my first three times on stage went pretty well. I thought I carried myself well, projected a fairly steady confidence, and moved fluidly from joke to joke. It was only when I looked back to the video that I noticed I was waving the microphone like I was trying to draw on my face, nervously pacing around the stage like a drunken madman, and getting more groans than laughs. It was pretty terrible. However, I did make one joke that got a small laugh. I reworked this bit to fit it into the joke structure, and I still use it (in its improved form) today. It's the same basic short story, but the small laugh is now a huge laugh rippling through a large audience.

Don't forget your lines.

Then there is the big fear: going blank on stage. Standing in front of an audience with no memory of what you're supposed to say is anxiety-inducing for even seasoned pros. The way to avoid this is to use a memory-recollection technique called the *memory palace*. Originally introduced in ancient Greek and Roman treatises, the memory palace premise is to create a place or a series of places in your mind where you can store information that you need to remember. In basic terms, it's a form of memory enhancement that uses visualization to organize and recall information.

Joshua Foer went on a year-long quest to improve his memory under the tutelage of top "mental athletes." Joshua began the year with a memory just like everybody else's. He finished that year as the 2006 USA Memory Champion.[31] In the book about his experiences, *Moonwalking with Einstein*, he explains:

> How we perceive the world and how we act in it are products of how and what we remember . . . No lasting joke, invention, insight, or work of art was ever produced by an external memory . . . Our ability to find humor in the world, to make connections between previously unconnected notions, to create new ideas, to share in a common culture: All these essentially human acts depend on memory.

One of the most useful and widely used mnemonic or memory aids Joshua learned to utilize is the memory palace, and he is not alone. Many memory contest champions claimed to use this technique in order to recall faces, digits, and listed words. These champions' successes have little to do with brain structure or intelligence, but more to do with the technique of using regions of their brain for specific learning. Or, in our case, remembering our material and avoiding the dreaded stage blank.

I was introduced to the power of the memory palace by San Francisco–based comedian Richard Sarvate. By night a very funny man, by day a more formal computer programmer at Yahoo!, he applies the same logic and rigor from his corporate office to his nightly adventures in comedy. When creating an image to put in your memory palace, he says, "It is useful to have the image interact with the environment. For my sushi joke I picture a sushi chef. If I put him in the elevator in the lobby of my apartment, I picture him mashing the buttons on the elevator in frustration. Now that he is interacting with the environment, it's a lot easier to visualize and recall. It's useful to make the image bizarre in order to make it more memorable. For my Mexican Indian joke I picture Krishna wearing a sombrero. A ridiculous image, which is almost tougher to forget."

The techniques Richard cites date back to sometime between 86 and 82 B.C. with the first Latin rhetoric textbook, *Rhetorica ad Herennium*, often referred to as the bible of mental athletes. The *ad Herennium*, Joshua outlines in his book, "advises readers at length about creating images for one's own memory palace: the funnier, lewder, and more bizarre, the better." We have known to use humor to be more memorable since before the Roman Empire, yet somewhere along the way, we forgot how. I guess someone in the Dark Ages forgot to picture Julius Caesar in his funny sheet toga.

How to craft your memory palace.

1. **Decide on a blueprint for your palace.** A memory palace can be a purely imagined place, but it's often easier to base it upon a place that exists in the real world, one that you are familiar with. The house you

grew up in, the apartment you're currently living in, and your office are all great examples.

2. **Define a route through this palace.** It's essential that you follow a specific route in a specific order through your palace so you'll log items in the order you want to speak about them.

3. **Identify specific storage locations in your palace and along your route.** This will give you defined places to store your information.

4. **Memorize the memory palace.** The best way to do this is by drawing out a blueprint so you can visualize it brought to life on paper, then create a memory in your mind.

5. **Place things to be remembered in your palace.** For example, if part of your presentation consists of talking about Ireland or a particular Irish guy you met (like me), do your best to create this person in as much detail as you can. This essentially burns an image in your mind that makes it easy to recall that element. The more humorous and absurd the better.

6. **Explore your palace and see everything you have created.** Visualize everything you have created and commit it to memory. Take a few moments to do this. These essentially become your practice run-throughs, in which you walk through the house and, along the way, encounter all the different memory points or key item topics for your presentation that you want to remember. If you go blank at any moment, stop and picture where you are in your memory palace.

For me, this is the lower floor of my house, with a path that takes in each room: I enter from the main door (the start of my talk), past key topic areas in each room, on the sofas, on the chairs, at the table, and then exit through the door (the conclusion of my talk). Using this technique, I have never gone blank on stage.

> Comedy and public speaking are a combination of what you say and how you say it. To say it best, you need to practice. Don't just turn up on the day and expect it to go well. Practice makes all the difference.

Remember, comedy and public speaking are a combination of what you say and how you say it. To say it best, you need to practice. Don't just turn up on the day and expect it to go well. Practice makes all the difference. And don't worry if the thought of going to an open mic or testing your material speaking in public scares you. There are plenty of ways to deal with stage fright.

Avoid stage fright.

Public speaking is generally listed as one of people's biggest fears. Stage fright is so common, it's easy to conjure up the image of what it looks like whether you have experienced it for yourself or not: a furiously pounding heart, shaking hands, sweaty palms, and all other manner of anxious, terrible, why-am-I-shivering nervousness. As I said earlier, it was my biggest fear. I thought it was a bad thing when I encountered all these involuntary reactions before speaking to an audience, but the more I looked into the psychology and science behind it, and the more I spoke to other comedians, performers, and presenters, the more I began to realize that this was perfectly normal.

This is my body's way of telling me that it is ready. The thought of negative consequences triggers glands to secrete the hormone ACTH. This hormone results in the release of adrenaline into your blood, and that's what causes these uncomfortable feelings. This is essentially your body's most alert and heightened state. It means you're ready. You want to focus on embracing this feeling. When you feel it, be happy. It means your body is in its peak condition to face a challenging or worrying situation.

Never seek to suppress this heightened state. One or two drinks or other substances before you publicly speak are never a good idea (a six-pack of Corona is even worse). Even one or two drinks can greatly suppress your body's reaction times and override a lot of these mechanisms designed to make us alert and perform better. Imagine you were a nervous racing car driver about to compete in a championship final decider. Naturally, you would feel very nervous. A shot of whiskey may seem like it could temporarily suppress those nerves, but would it be a good idea? Not unless you like crashes.

When faced with stage fright, it's helpful to remember a tip from the business world—the 5 Ps: Proper Planning Prevents Poor Performance. When it comes time to take the stage, trust your training. You have put in the work and you are ready. Chances are, it's going to go really well. Close your eyes and try and hear your own heart beat before you go on stage. Breathe and relax. Stretching is also a great and widely used technique. Stretching sends out hormones to trigger a relaxation response in your body. I hate stretching and yoga, to be honest. I am far too ADD. The one time you will find me doing it, however, is just before I walk on stage. It makes a huge difference!

Steve Martin knew all too well how many things could go wrong in a single performance: "Stand-up is seldom performed in ideal circumstances. Comedy's enemy is distraction, and rarely do comedians get a pristine performing environment. I worried about the sound system, ambient noise, hecklers, drunks, lighting, sudden clangs, latecomers, and loud talkers, not to mention the nagging concern 'Is this funny?' "

He also knew that his fears could be put to his advantage: "I suppose these worries keep the mind sharp and the senses active. I can remember instantly retiming a punch line to fit around the crash of a dropped glass of wine or raising my voice to cover a patron's ill-timed sneeze, seemingly microseconds before the interruption happened."[32]

For Martin, it was practice and stage time (no matter how excruciating) that made all the difference as he improved his comedic performance. Practice is the key to a strong performance in both the best- and worst-case scenarios. Over-preparation will help you be ready for anything. The knowledge and confidence that you can handle whatever comes your way on stage will assuage some of the fear you might be feeling. All of the practice will be well worth it. With calm nerves, rehearsed delivery, and material you know through and through, you will look better on stage than you could ever hope to without consistent practice. After all, as Steve Martin says, "Persistence is a great substitute for talent."

Exercise: Hone Your Stories and Build a Set List

Find a space at home or work and tell your stories while recording them. This can be audio or video recorded. Video is better, if possible. Don't stop to make corrections. This is where you vocalize thoughts and let your mind wander. You'll be surprised what little additions you tend to make compared to your writing.

A strange thing happens when we are forced to vocalize a story. We tend to feel the need to fill the silence, even with no audience present. In doing so we add a lot of filler words, but also, importantly, many additional details we may not have put in written form. This conscious vocalization can also save you a lot of stage time.

Listen back to see if you made any additions worth keeping and also identify where you can cut words. Note any differences between how you told the story versus how you wrote it back in the exercise from chapter two. Often this can be a great way to refine your words and find extra small details that can make a big difference to your tale.

If your story makes you laugh even a little on listening back, then you have something good to work with. If you love telling a story, it's likely others will love to listen.

Now rewrite what you like best, following the joke structure outlined earlier.

Take your favorite stories and cut them down to the fewest possible words to compile a five-minute set list. Your set list is simply a list of topics/stories you intend to try out on stage, usually listed by key words. (No need to write out every word. Think more along the lines of a postcard with bullet points.)

Work from these bullet points to create your own memory palace. For those of you who intend to try stand-up comedy, five minutes is likely the amount of time you will get initially at an open mic night (three to seven minutes is the range you get as a beginner, with five the most common). Many of you have no intention of ever attending an open mic night or simply don't have the time, which is completely fine. For you, this set list should be items you practice on real people whether at work or outside it.

As you attend more public speaking events or build up to trying them, your set list should get longer as you continuously add new material that you know works. Typically, a new comedian can produce five to seven strong minutes within the first few months, a professional comedian sixty new minutes a year. Remember, you only need a few strong jokes and not a full five to seven minutes to liven up your presentation. However, the longer your "comedy set" becomes (should you be brave enough and have the time to try it), the more tried and trusted jokes you will have to build into your public speaking/presentations.

Watch Joe Kowan's TED talk on the subject of stage fright, titled "How I Beat Stage Fright."

Delivery

"I never memorize a speech verbatim, but I do ensure that I have memorized the starting and closing 2–3 sentences for each portion."

–Tim Ferriss

"All right, who's next?" The open mic host stood at the foot of the stage, shading his eyes against the light as he looked toward some unseen list-keeper. My heart starts to pound because I already know the answer.

"Dave," a voice from the crowd says. "That's all it says, though . . . Dave."

Was I supposed to write my last name? The sheet wasn't specific. I stand up from my seat and raise my hand. *What are you doing?* I asked myself. *You're not a child answering roll call.* I lower my hand in what I hope was a casual move. A cool, calm, relaxed, casual move. Better add a flick of the wrist for good measure. A cool, calm, relaxed, casual fly swat.

"What's your last name, Dave?" the host asks, motioning me to step forward.

"Ehhh . . . Nihill." That was my name, right? As I walk toward him I was at least 72 percent sure that it was.

"Do you want to use it in your introduction? Or do you prefer to be a mystery Dave?"

"Thanks very much, I'll take it." I step up the small rise of the stage.

"Do you want me to introduce you as Dave Michael or just Dave?"

"David Nihill," I say as I step to the mic. "Michael is a whole new name."

"Please give it up for George Michael!"

Great.

This was my very first attempt at stand-up—now you see why using the stage name "Irish Dave" had quick appeal. This awkward conversation played out live on stage. The joke at my expense got me off to the worst possible start. I had already sweated out my T-shirt and began to fumble with my notes. Shakin' Stevens was well and truly in the house as my struggles to control my adrenaline greatly reduced my ability to do something as simple as take the microphone out of the stand. Within seconds, my mind went blank and I was reading from a sheet of paper I struggled to hold steady. As I paced the stage nervously, I completely forgot to keep the mic near my mouth and waved it around like an extension of my arm. The audience probably became concerned that my windmill arms would eventually whip the mic into my head, dropping me into merciful unconsciousness. Every gesticulation increased that possibility—thereby greatly reducing the likelihood I would get any laughs, as the audience waited for the telltale thud that would put an end to my miserable state.

It never got any better that night. I didn't bounce back. And here's the crazy thing: this was not a grand theater stage, a large conference, or a new product launch. This was the half-completed basement of an Irish bar, the state of which appeared like there was a breakdown in communications between Irish contractors and Mexican laborers (or vice versa). There must have been no more than eight people there. EIGHT people! What was happening to me?

As I have learned the hard way, your behavior on stage will greatly impact your performance. Comedians are the true masters of public speaking delivery, and a lot can be learned from things they do quite naturally but have often learned in rather painful ways. In this chapter, we are going to look at a number of key techniques to be aware of when it comes time to pick up the mic and speak real words into it. Needless to say, I really wish I knew all these prior to my spectacular debut.

Start Strong/First 30

As any 100-meter sprinter knows, it's much harder to win if you get off to a weak start. Likewise, the first thirty seconds of your presentation can determine the rest of your talk. You want to start off well or it will affect your performance as easily as a sprinter's slow time off the block. The first thirty seconds is your time to grab the audience's attention. Tell them who you are, why they must listen to you, and do it in a manner that makes them like you. I have had nights where I have told the exact same jokes and stories but with very different reactions. The nights that did not go as well were the ones in which I experimented with or messed up the first thirty seconds. Keep in mind that if the first thirty seconds will set the tone for the rest of your talk (they will), you must rehearse this thirty seconds the most.

> **The first thirty seconds is your time to grab the audience's attention. Tell them who you are, why they must listen to you, and do it in a manner that makes them like you.**

The structure of the First 30 is important. Steve Jobs always saved the best for last with, "One more thing," and you should, too. Include your second-best joke at the start and leave your best until the end to go out with the strongest impression possible. I will show you later in the book how to identify and evaluate your best bits, jokes, and stories.

Picture yourself in this scenario. It's Friday morning. You send out an email to all your friends, colleagues, and anyone even remotely connected to your professional career. "Hey, so, I am putting on this thing at the office and I think you should come. It will start with me reading aloud my prior work experience in chronological order. I will do my best to give a heightened sense of importance to my own contributions, like reading a résumé. Some of you, unknown to me, may have even used LinkedIn to endorse me for said contributions even though you have slight knowledge, at best, of who I am. I will not solicit or incorporate opinions of yours. But the information I shall recite shall be already known to most of you. The host may touch on it and you may come across it in official material leading up to said event. There will be no alcohol served, as this is a professional event. Who's in?" Very few is the answer, yet most business presentations start in this manner. Choose not to.

As I learned the hard way, don't leave your introduction to chance. Your talk starts with your introduction. It's your chance to have the host list why you are qualified to be there, why the audience should listen to you, and essentially list your achievements so you don't have to. This allows you to start with a story rather than a self-promotional chronological ordering of your achievements, however big or small. Word it so your name is said only once and as the very last words. This gives the audience their cue to applaud as your name is mentioned, but also builds anticipation to who you might be. Always supply an introduction in advance. And for the love of breathing, don't forget to include your last name. Many hosts or emcees try to improvise humorous interludes themselves. Don't let their laughs be at your expense. George Michael wouldn't . . . or would he?

Get on stage fast.

As soon as the host introduces you (hopefully this will be accompanied with a round of applause), quickly make your way onto the stage. You should be in position to commence speaking as soon as the applause begins to dwindle. If, for any reason, you need to set up or adjust some items at this point, it's a great moment to ask the audience for a round of applause for your host or previous speaker.

Applause also follows the Rule of 3. It essentially gets the audience into the habit of applauding and laughing. If the host didn't introduce you with a strong round of applause, this is a good time for you to ask the audience to offer one. If you do this in groups of three, it's more likely that their applause will spill over and become a habit that stays evident for the rest of your presentation and for others to follow. For example, you can ask for a round of applause for the presenter, the host, for some of the presenters before you, or for the sponsor or organizers of the show/conference/talk.

Smile and make eye contact.

Connect with as many people as you can in the front rows for the duration of this first thirty seconds and as much as you can throughout the rest of your talk. This helps you to engage as many members of the audience as you can on a personal level. If you look like you're enjoying it and you look happy, chances are other people will start to as well.

Try and get a quick laugh.

Luis von Ahn is a Guatemalan entrepreneur and an associate computer science professor at Carnegie Mellon University. More annoyingly to the average Internet user, he is the inventor of CAPTCHA, that frustrating sequence of barely visible letters that prevents you accessing your email, bank account, or drunkenly making surprise Amazon purchases for yourself at times you really need to. Addressing the audience at TEDx, he started by acknowledging the likely feelings of the crowd toward his fine work and also flipped their expectations by leading them expertly into a laugh line: "How many of you have had to fill out some sort of web form where you have been asked to read a distorted sequence of characters like this? Yep. How many found it really, really annoying? Okay, outstanding. So, I invented that."

The result: An immediate attention-grabbing start with a strong laugh as he rapidly humanized his work. A great example of starting strong.

Over the course of my experiment I tested many different opening lines. Here is one from October 2014 at the San Jose Improv Comedy Club: "You think a foreign accent in the US would be a good thing . . . until you realize nobody can understand you. Try calling one of your automated customer service lines with this accent. 'Thank you for calling Bank of America. For English press one. Para Español, marque número dos. If you're Irish, just send us an email.' "

There is always a tension in the room as the audience tries to figure out a little bit about you and decides if they want to listen to you. Getting a quick laugh can be a great way to lighten the mood. Move forward from there with an anecdote or a personal story. This should establish affinity with your audience. It should tell them who you are, what your passion is, and why they should have your passion, too, whether it's about a product or research area or a topic in general. This should be relevant and engaging and have the key elements of a good story as outlined in Comedy Habit #1: Start with a Story. The dopamine released with those early laughs will immediately put the audience and you more at ease; this will further drive engagement and break down barriers. Picturing the room naked is useful if you're so inclined, but making the naked people laugh is a lot more interesting.

> "Picturing the room naked is useful if you're so inclined, but making the naked people laugh is a lot more interesting."

Nudity aside, acknowledging the obvious often provides an opportunity to get a quick and early laugh. If you're visibly nervous, have a fresh stain on your shirt, or if there's anything unusual about you physically—anything that the audience might fixate on at the start—now is the time to address it, get a laugh, and move on so the audience can focus. In my case, I have an Irish accent that stands out because I live in the United States. I will work to quickly address this by telling them that I'm Irish and trying to build a joke about it. That way, I can get the audience to focus on what I'm saying rather than spend the first thirty seconds trying to figure out where I'm from.

Calling the Room

Acknowledging the obvious is known in comedy as "calling the room." It means vocalizing exactly what's going on in the room or what people are likely thinking. When Twitter launched, cofounder Biz Stone was keen for the company to own its many early-stage imperfections—most notably the fact that the system was completely unreliable. When you sent a message on most websites, a success screen came up that would have read, "Thank you. Your message was sent." Twitter merely left you with a message that said, "Great, that might have worked."

Acknowledging the feelings of a room of people you can see is a lot easier than predicting those on the other side of a screen. We get real-time visual feedback and the best speakers capitalize on it. Vocalize everything that's happening in that moment, everything that is being shared between you and the audience. It can be comments on lunch, the setup, the room temperature, someone arriving late or leaving early, a loud noise, someone sneezing, a fire alarm going off in the background, et cetera. Comedians never ignore these moments as they often generate spontaneous laughs. The more you try calling the room, the better you get at it, and the more you know what works well, the more potential occurrences you can address and the better rehearsed this spontaneity becomes.

One of my clients opened his keynotes by playing a video that highlighted his considerable list of business and personal achievements—all of the things that earned him a net worth of more than $400 million. The video, although hugely impressive and very well made, really put him up on a pedestal. It made people find him hard to instantly relate to and not very likable. Then he tried to tell some jokes, and the reception was exactly what you would expect. If you don't like someone, you are unlikely to laugh at their jokes no matter how funny they may be. It was time for some damage control. I asked him to come out on stage after the video and say, "Does it show my mother made that video? If my wife had made it, it would look very different!" He had to laugh at himself so the audience would laugh with him. With this use of self-deprecating humor, he was suddenly very human again. His presentation jokes now got bigger laughs.

Self-deprecating humor can be one of the quickest ways to get an audience on your side. According to a recent *Financial Times* article by Lucy Kellaway, self-deprecation can "disarm others, make them forget you are scarily powerful, and lull them into liking you,"[33] but it only works if you're already in a position of power and authority. Self-deprecating humor is a great tool to have in your back pocket, but be sure not to undermine your own credibility with too many wisecracks or humorous comments at your own expense.

To quote Jerry Seinfeld again, "No one is more judged in civilized society than a stand-up comedian. Every twelve seconds, you're rated."[34] It's not as bad for us in this context for presentations, but the first thirty seconds are ones we need to get right. Practice this part the most. Make no bones about it, this opening period is a popularity contest and one you need to win.

Helpful Tip:

Try and introduce yourself to as many people in the room as possible before you start to speak. It helps break down that initial barrier that a stage can create. Don't wait until you have already addressed the audience to start working the room.

On-Stage Delivery

Now, a few things to keep in mind for not only the first thirty seconds, but throughout your talk.

Speak up—not "ah," "eh," "but."

It sounds straightforward enough, but make sure you speak loud enough for people to hear you. You need to reach everybody in the room. The added benefit is that by speaking as little as 20 percent louder than normal, you will reduce the amount of filler words ("ah," "eh," "but") you tend to use. It's hard to say "eh" or "em" with this higher-than-normal tone. This feels strange to do but sounds perfectly normal to your audience.

Don't eat the microphone.

This should fall under the "instinct" category, but you can't be sure with people these days. Don't underestimate what your nerves might drive you to do. New comics and new presenters tend to keep it a little bit too close to their mouth. Keep it a good distance away from your mouth; ideally, keep it down by your chin. When I am really nervous, I leave the mic in the stand until I get a few early laughs and feel more confident. Then once the nerves have calmed, I move the stand out of the way.

Trust yourself and your material.

If you look like you know what you're doing, people will believe it and that confidence is infectious. Remember, people are fundamentally good at heart. Nobody wants to see a speaker or performer doing badly. They want to see you succeed. Give them reason to think you will.

Speak instead of preach.

Try as much as you can to be conversational on stage and avoid preaching. This relaxes the audience and makes it seem more of a spontaneous discussion.

Make sure you are fully visible.

If there's a podium, try to get out from behind it. If there's a mic stand, once you're comfortable, take the mic out and move the stand to one side. Often the audience needs to see you to fully trust you.

Mind your face.

Your expression is incredibly important from the moment you step on stage to the moment you walk off. Remember to smile. Make eye contact with as many people as you can. Try and build connections.

Use your hands.

Remember to use those hands, and make sure you leave the practice bottles at home. Moving your hands more increases your chances of your talk going viral. Giving your talk while double-fisting drinks pretty much guarantees it. Your call. As comedian Matt Morales advised on this one, "Choosing the latter might not make your presentation better, but eventually you won't care anymore."

Don't pet the hamster.

New and experienced speakers alike tend to couple their hands nervously in front of their body almost as if they are petting a cute little hamster. Leave the hamster at home and consciously catch yourself every time you stroke the imaginary little furball.

Use the stage.

If you have a large stage area to work with, use it to reach people. Connect with them by walking toward them and covering as much of the stage area as you can. Be careful not to nervously sprint around the place. You don't want to distract them or take away from what you're saying.

Amp up your punch line.

When you come to the punch line of your joke or the important laugh line, step forward and raise your voice. This combination really emphasizes a point and will further engage the audience. It also gives them their cue to laugh.

Don't bring visible notes on stage with you.

Podiums are becoming a thing of the past as most organizers realize they create a barrier between the speaker and audience, so sooner or later you'll have nowhere to put them. It's best not to rely on them at all, but if you must have something, be sneaky about it. Write a few notes on a water bottle label or a napkin. Notes should stay in your back pocket throughout. If you don't have a back pocket, get creative. Visible notes show the audience that you're not fully prepared and also force you to break flow and eye contact.

Close your wardrobe.

Nervous sweating is just something that happens from time to time. With this in mind, always wear dark colors and fabrics that don't show sweat patches on stage. Steve Jobs was known for his black turtleneck uniform. It meant one less thing he had to worry about in life. I applied the same theory to public speaking. Knowing what to wear every time I took the stage (and knowing that the sweaty circles collecting over my body would stay my little secret) meant one less thing to worry about. Make sure your presentation wardrobe includes fabrics like 100 percent cotton, linen, lightweight merino wool, jersey, chambray, rayon, silk, or moisture-wick fabric.

Don't forget to pause.

Timing, rhythm, and pauses become really important. While delivery is how you say a joke, timing is *when* you say it. A proper pause can help create curiosity within an audience. Give them a chance to catch their breath, build tension, and then, BANG! You burst into the laugh line. These pauses and rhythms essentially give the audience entrance into your train of thought, allowing a true reaction to build. Small changes in delivery like raising your voice at the end of a sentence have a big, big impact. Comedians say there is no substitute for stage time to improve timing. While this is true in part, what mainly happens over time is that one masters the delivery of tested stories and laugh lines. When I identified my best stories and bits to include and the exact parts that generally get laughs, I was more confident in adjusting my delivery to allow time for the audience to laugh. I am expecting them to laugh and, in facilitating this laugh, my timing improves.

Improvisation

"You can't plan a script. The beauty of improvisation is you're experiencing it in the moment," says former Twitter CEO Dick Costolo who, long before his role at Twitter, performed for years as an improv comedian in Chicago alongside the likes of Steve Carell as part of the famous improv group, Second City.[35]

Riffing is when a comedian interacts with an audience by asking them questions, either to the group as a whole or an individual, making stuff up on the spot and appearing as spontaneous as can be. This is essentially improv comedy, which in the context of performing arts is spontaneous performance without specific preparation. Improv often gets the biggest laughs as it appears to occur truly in the moment and creates an in-joke between the speaker and the audience. It can often also add an element of magic or creativity that didn't seem apparent in preparation. The most effective comedians combine stand-up, storytelling, and improv techniques. The best business presenters should, too. Don't be afraid to go off script once you have gotten a good, scripted start.

> "Real laughter is spontaneous. Like water from the spring it bubbles forth a creation of mingled action and spontaneity—two magic potions in themselves—the very essence of laughter—the unrestrained emotion within us!"
> **–Douglas Fairbanks**

In *Raiders of the Lost Ark*, improv led to one of the movie's most memorable scenes, in which Indiana Jones, played by Harrison Ford, is confronted by a skilled swordsman. The scene became the movie's biggest laugh line, but it wasn't planned that way. Ford was defeated by the local cuisine (like me in Guatemala). Lacking the energy for the fight scene shot in Tunisia's intense heat, he improvised. Rather than use his sword as scripted by Steven Spielberg, he simply took out his gun and shot the would-be assassin. The unplanned scene became an instant classic. Improv has the power to do that.

Knowing the room and the audience can really help you tailor material and certain jokes to that particular crowd's interest. It can be advantageous if you can get a list of attendees before your conference or presentation and determine where the majority has come from, their average age, job titles, et cetera. If a lot traveled to be there, come from a specific company, or hail from a particular country, it's good to reference this in your presentation and work in some jokes when you can.

"Improv teaches you how to think on your feet and how to react and adapt very quickly to unexpected events."
–Lakshmi Balachandra

Watch speakers that go on before you, so you can build on their jokes or find spontaneous ways to reference them if you can. This will also help you make sure you're not overlapping with any of your material or main points. It always amazes me how many business speakers and comedians don't do this. Their rationale is often that they don't want their own planned talk affected by what they see before them, but if someone goes on before you and covers very similar topics and makes similar jokes, the benefits outweigh the costs. Audiences often get an overload of information in a short time span. With this in mind, don't call back too far. A good rule is to keep your references within the last three performers (i.e., if you are the sixth to speak, only work back to the third act). If you reference something that was said a day earlier, the audience will likely not recall it fast enough.

What if a joke falls flat? This is going to happen sometimes no matter how good the joke. It's great to call attention to it if it does. Vocalize what the audience members are thinking. If a joke didn't go well, acknowledge it and quickly move on, saying, "Oh, boy, that one didn't go too well. Just as well, I've got a better one," and move on to it. Or, "You guys didn't like that one? My dog loved it! I've been practicing on him," and tell something else. Always acknowledge what seems to be the mood of the audience. If something didn't work, show that audience that you realize it and they will forgive you.

At the same San Francisco location where comedian Zach Galifianakis (aka Alan from the movie *The Hangover*) shot to fame, Jeff Kreisler took the stage and displayed a line like this to great effect. Jeff is winner of the Bill Hicks Spirit Award for Thought Provoking Comedy, bestselling author, TEDx speaker, and Comedy Central writer. While testing out a new joke, he didn't quite get the reaction he wanted from the crowd. Jeff faced the audience with a pondering glance, paused a moment, as if lost in profound thought, and then unleashed the words, "Wow, as an audience, you guys really laugh . . . sparingly." The resulting laughter was anything but.

If you do happen to forget your next line, even though you've used the memory palace technique, don't worry. Just be honest and say, "I forgot my next line," if you have. Take your time and it will come to you. Try and bring a bottle or a glass of water on stage with you. This will allow you to take a drink and take a break if, at any moment, you forget exactly where you are in your talk or memory palace. Remember, you can always have fun with the situation. You can always say something humorous and sarcastic to acknowledge that it's not going so well: "You guys may think I'm doing badly. Not true. You're doing badly. Go home and study and really prepare for these audience appearances."

By working out your rescue lines ahead of time, you can step over these small issues without missing a beat in your delivery.

Even when you're improvising it's important to remember your comic writing tips: keep to the present tense and bring this to life in your delivery. Your attitude can be a great help as well. Use attitude words and deliver with attitude. Really sell your topic, stories, and jokes like they're important to you. Remember to incorporate words like *weird*, *scary*, *amazing*, *hard*, *stupid*, *crazy*, and *nuts*. It's easy to forget them in the moment.

Delivery is the part where you will improve the most in the shortest period of time. Some lessons may be temporarily painful, but they will be easily remembered and likely avoided in the future. Like when I was seven years old and I was fishing for tadpoles down next to a river. I took a break to urinate without surveying my surroundings. When the electrical current from the fence made its ways to my private parts, I learned a very good lesson. Check before you spray. It was a lesson I only needed to learn once. The lessons ingrained from experience, much like those that come through storytelling, are always easily recalled to guide our future behavior.

Outside of checking before you urinate on electrically charged devices, the items I've described may sound like a lot to remember. That's because they are. Just like a soccer player coming back from injury or a boxer who has gone awhile without a fight, there is a noticeable difference in combining all these items when you haven't been on stage for too long.

Delivery needs to be practiced. When I have a big show or I am hosting a conference, I make sure to put in some practice time a few days before to iron out the kinks. Even the best, most veteran comedians still do this. Jerry Seinfeld still travels around the United States to perform regularly at smaller venues. He told the *New York Times*:

> If I don't do a set in two weeks I feel it. I read an article a few years ago that said when you practice a sport a lot, you literally become a broadband: the nerve pathway in your brain contains a lot more information. As soon as you stop practicing, the pathway begins shrinking back down. Reading that changed my life. I used to wonder, Why am I doing these sets, getting on a stage? Don't I know how to do this already? The answer is no. You must keep doing it. The broadband starts to narrow the moment you stop.[36]

Just like Steve Martin and Jerry Seinfeld do, the best business speakers take every opportunity to build muscle memory and keep the nerve pathways at their most effective by practicing their delivery. You should, too.

Just one more thing . . .

Have fun with this. It's a creative process, and, just like learning any creative process, you'll only get better from here. The more you enjoy it—and look like you are enjoying it— the more the crowd will, too. They look to you to craft their behaviors, like an orchestra taking their cues from a conductor. Think less Shakin' Stevens and more Steve Jobs. Always save the best for last.

Exercise: Practice Time

Try and develop an opening line, bearing in mind the importance of the first thirty seconds of a talk. This exercise is taken from an article by best-selling author and comedy coach Judy Carter:

Make a list of your ethnicity, your parents' nationalities, your hobbies, and your current and past professions.

Pick two of the items you wrote and insert them into the following formula:

"You may not know this, but I'm _____ and _____ (or "I'm part this and part that"), so that means I _____."

By doing this you are seeking to identify key attributes about yourself and communicate them to the audience in a humorous manner. Much in the same way I reference my Irish accent in my opening line and acknowledge folks may be having a hard time understanding me.

Try and speak publicly this week. Give a work presentation, speak up in your next lecture, ask a question at a talk, or volunteer to speak at a school or coworking space. If up to now you have been practicing at home in your underpants, it would be better still if you can get on stage by finding an open mic night (and of course something to cover those sexy legs) or storytelling night (like The Moth) near you. Prior to going, select and make plans to attend a second one within two weeks if possible. This serves to commit you to going again regardless of how you do at your first one. If you really, really don't want to try an open mic to start with, look up your local Toastmasters group or find a public speaking meetup. If even that sounds too much, practice on friends and family until you know you have the makings of a good story, then progress to stages as soon as you can. There really is no substitute for testing stories and humorous anecdotes on a live audience.

Get into the habit of speaking publicly at events, work, and/or open mics. You don't have to go all the time. The more serious your aspirations as a speaker, the higher your time commitment. Once every two weeks is a good start.

Reward yourself after each talk, not before. This can be as simple as watching TV, going for a run, or snorting a piece of chocolate. (Don't judge me. Nerves can do strange things.) Positive reinforcement helps you establish a habit as well as it helped teach your dog that rollover trick you're so proud of.

No drinking or other substances prior to your performance. You want to fully embrace your heightened state of alertness.

Keep most material and stories clean. It needs to be usable in a business context. As a rule of thumb, if it's below the waist, leave it out.

Try to incorporate one act-out into your story.

Try hard whether your audience is three or three thousand people. The same rules apply.

Practice, practice, and practice and remember to record by audio or video.

For the times you get on stage, watch and listen to your recorded performances. Highlight:

- What got a reaction from your audience?
- What held people's attention?
- What got laughs?
- What areas can you take out or rewrite?
- How was your body language and delivery on stage?
- What areas do you need to work on?

Delivery circumstances change. Jokes and stories can get a good reaction one time and little reaction the next. Sometimes this can be due to other factors like the height of the stage and ceiling in the room, the amount of natural light, how attentive the crowd was, the mood/setup in the venue, the performer before you, your opening thirty seconds, et cetera.

Before you cut a joke or story from your planned set, make sure that you test it at least three times, especially if you really like telling it. Remember it can be tough to get laughs at some venues. Even a small chuckle can translate to big laughs in your final presentation to a larger, more attentive audience (and especially a business audience).

Look into taking an improv class near you. At the time of writing, Twitter holds up to four a week at their corporate headquarters. There's a good reason why they do, and it's a great excuse to give your boss if you need to. You'll even get extra points for quoting MIT: a study there found a group of improv comedians generated 20 percent more ideas than professional product designers did.[37] Practicing improv comedy develops your ability to create, just as practice improves your writing or speaking ability. It's a genuinely valuable exercise.

Be aware of body language. Watch Amy Cuddy's TED talk on the subject, "Body Language Shapes Who You Are," if you have not seen it before.

Many a time I have seen comedians crush it on stage without cracking a smile, moving their hands or even looking up at the audience. Body language is very important, but rubbish content delivered beautifully is still rubbish.

Control the Audience

"The smart way to keep people passive and obedient
is to strictly limit the spectrum of acceptable opinion,
but allow very lively debate within that spectrum."
—Noam Chomsky

What Stanford is to universities, a perfectly set-up room in downtown San Francisco is to comedy. The Punchline Comedy Club has low ceilings that help laughter bounce around the room; lots of red coloring, which scientists say is more conducive to laughter; tightly packed seating, which helps spread emotions; and a stage that sits low and almost within the crowd. A joke here will get a bigger laugh than most other venues. Comedians love performing here, and, just like Stanford, only the better ones get in. For a new comedian, the best chance of taking the stage there is the venue's Sunday night showcase. The rules for the showcase are unwritten, but generally you are expected to have been doing comedy for at least two years, come to the show most Sundays for nine months, and patiently wait to be called on to deliver your best seven minutes to a packed house. Patience is not my strong suit and shortcuts are my specialty. During my year's experiments I managed to get on stage at the Punchline seven times. But tonight it's not someone developing his craft and trying his luck as a comedian with a pretty tragic stage name. Tonight it's Andrew. He has honed his craft over ten years as a full-time touring comedian, and he is incredibly good at making audiences double over in laughter while dominating a room. Andrew finds a couple in the audience.

"Now here's a good-looking couple. How long have you two been together?"

"Two years," the man answers while his lady friend leans in affectionately.

"What's your name?"

"John."

"Is it serious, John?"

"Yes."

John's girlfriend is blushing. She's also extremely pleased. She glances at him affectionately, and she's not the only one. This room full of strangers is now getting to know and like John and his pretty girlfriend.

"Good-looking girl. You probably know after a year together. Do you love her?"

"Yes," John answers quickly. Smartly.

"Well done, John. He knows the rules. No matter what the question, never hesitate. Do you love her? Yes. Is she fat? No. Bang . . . Never hesitate. Good work. You are getting the good loving tonight."

The audience laughs, the girl laughs, and John laughs, knowing he nailed this impromptu test.

"So, it's a serious relationship. Are you engaged?"

"No." John looks like he has swallowed something sharp.

"So it's serious, she is amazing, you're very happy. You love her. It's a great relationship. You can tell. Serious. Some people would say very serious. But . . . it's not engagement serious, John . . . Not engagement serious. Look at all the ladies. They loved you before when you said you love her but now they are asking, 'Why not, John? Why not engaged?' Do you know what would make this an amazing night, John? Do you know what would make this extremely memorable for both of you?"

The anticipation and tension builds and becomes nervous laughter. Is Andrew really going to ask him to propose to his girlfriend in front of a room of strangers?

"Look at John's face. You should see it. He's like, 'Joke's over, asshole. Move on now.'

Don't worry John. We wouldn't do that. I wouldn't make you ask in front of all these people." Andrew turns to the girl, "But, if he did ask, what would you say, John's girlfriend?"

"Yes . . ." the girl says softly.

"Wow." Andrew looks up, "Oh, sorry John. I have just ruined your life."

This joke looks every bit spontaneous and in the moment. And it is, but it was very much in the moment with a different couple the previous night as well, and the night before that. This is the essence of rehearsed spontaneity combined with controlling the audience. Andrew has put in a lot of work and analysis behind the scenes to test out various formats and wording to lead into this core joke premise. This moment that seems so spontaneous is mostly anything but.

The best comedians and presenters have topics in mind that they are well prepared on and wish to discuss. The mastery in their delivery comes from steering the audience in the right direction to arrive at just what they had planned to talk about. Can this be done regularly? It can. Remember, you have the microphone. You control the room. This also applies to interviews and all social interactions. As a speaker, you can control how much the audience member speaks with the type of questions you ask. If you're trying to engage the audience members and you want them to talk for a longer period of time, ask open, leading questions. Use words like *how*, *who*, *when*, *what*, *why*, and *where* to elicit a response greater than one word. They generally require some further explanation. If you want to appear to be engaging an audience member, but don't want them to speak that much, ask a closed question, one that tends to solicit yes-or-no or other one-word answers.

> You need to make the audience like you, but you also need to be able to control them collectively, as they will decide collectively if they want to listen to you.

Something strange happens when you put a group of people who previously didn't know each other together in a room. They begin to react together, to laugh together, and to applaud together. They essentially begin to behave as one. You need to present to them like you're constantly seeking their approval. This goes back to the previous comedy lesson. You need to make the audience like you, but you also need to be able to control them collectively, as they will decide collectively if they want to listen to you.

Command Attention

So many times I have seen a business speaker take the stage and begin to talk while the audience is still chatting or not quite settled. Sometimes it's the result of the host not doing his or her job, and sometimes it's due to a range of other factors, but one thing is certain: you need to stop the noise. The speaker all too often tolerates the crowd's chatter, puts their head down and seeks to plough through their presentation as fast as they can. What happens? The noise level gets higher and higher.

Next time this happens, stop and ask the audience to clap if they can hear you. Once a few begin to clap, keep it going until those who were talking shut up and join in. They will. Like birds flocking together, people naturally behave as a group. They will assume you said something interesting worthy of applause, fear they missed something awesome, and join in. Now you reset and start again. I run a conference series and this is how I commence every time. It never fails. "Clap if you can hear me."

Never Ignore Interruptions, Always Manage Disruptions

Sooner or later you'll be interrupted in a talk or presentation. In a comedy show this is referred to as heckling. These unwanted interruptions will disrupt your flow, but they should be endured until it's clear that the audience is also annoyed. You'll begin to feel this. When you do, then you can close off the intruder with the audience's implicit approval. We can all recall times presenting, when somebody kept going on and on without really getting to the point of the question. If this was annoying you, it was probably annoying the audience as well. Just make sure it's actually happening before closing them off. Always be polite unless you really, really have no other option. Remember, you control the audience. You have the microphone and your voice will be considerably louder than anybody else's in the room no matter how much they shout.

Few comebacks from the comedy stage are appropriate for use in a business context, but there is no harm in learning from some more extreme examples, then adapting a more light-hearted version.

Ricky Gervais: *"This is a big venue, I can't really get into one-to-ones. In a smaller room I'd still ignore you—Shut up!"*

Arthur Smith: *"Look, it's all right to donate your brain to science, but shouldn't you have waited 'til you died?"*

Rufus Hound (to waitstaff): *"Can we get some crayons and a menu for this guy to color in, please?"*

Often the best way to deal with an intrusion or comment is simply to repeat that comment. If it was an obviously stupid question, by simply repeating it and pausing for effect the audience will likely laugh spontaneously. This repeat serves a number of purposes. First and most important, it buys you time to think. This extra time allows you to come up either with something witty and spontaneous or the best answer to their question, comment, or concern. You can often get easy laughs here by intentionally mispronouncing a certain word within their question. For example, an audience member asks, "You said the key number was 10 percent in your talk. Can you clarify, because she said in her report that it's 30 percent." The speaker replies, "A *sheep* said it's 30 percent. Those sheep can't be trusted. I would strongly encourage you to avoid quoting sheep, especially at business events like this one. Those sheep are no good with numbers: one, two, three, four, zzzzzz . . . They're asleep . . . oh, *she,* you said. Sorry, my apologies. It's always hard when the audience are much smarter than I." The apology line here, much like Jeff accusing the audience of "laughing sparingly" in the last chapter, is a backup in case the audience member looks offended. It flips the original joke, at their expense, now back to one at your own, and serves to get the audience back on your side. Often you could just as easily move on to the next question without using it. It all depends on how that particular group reacts. Something you will get better and better at judging, the more you are on stage.

Misunderstood questions are often a common occurrence, and whether you are making light of them or not, make sure that everybody in the room heard the question. Repeat it. You can always add, "That's a great question," if you need more time. Constantly seek to buy time to think on your feet. There's no hurry to give an answer. Don't be afraid of silence. Silence means the audience is listening to you.

For instance, a geeky-looking comedian says, "This is how bad I was at sex the first time. The first time I ever had sex—"

"Yesterday?" yells a heckler. The audience responds with huge laughter.

The comedian visibly struggles to find words as the audience continues to laugh for a full twenty-nine seconds. Finally, he looks at his heckler and says, "Glad you remember." The room swells with even bigger laughs as the audience goes wild in approval. (Watch at https://www.youtube.com/watch?v=54AW7V2O9xc.)

There's no rush to craft your response. The best answer or comeback is worth taking the time to put together.

Never Run the Clock

The easiest way to lose an audience is to exceed your allocated time limit, what comedians call running the clock. Comedians are better at respecting this than anyone else. Why? Because in comedy, if you run the clock you will not be allowed on stage again at that location. In no club or venue will it be tolerated unless you're an A-list headliner. There are more than fifty thousand people who call themselves comedians in the United States. All of them over time become pretty funny. Not all will be hilarious and make the big time. In fact, very few will. All, however, will learn this one great lesson along the way: never run the clock.

Practice your timing and aim to never, ever go over the allocated time limit. If there isn't a set time limit to go by, make sure that you impose one on yourself. This forces you to go back and strip out any unnecessary words or information and be a minimalist. Use the fewest words with the greatest impact.

If you're due to speak for ten minutes, this time period becomes essentially a nonverbal agreement with the audience. In their mind, if they expect you to speak for ten minutes, then they're already planning on doing something else in ten minutes' time, whether that's catching up on some work email, going to the bathroom, or grabbing some lunch. It'll be much harder for you to hold their attention if you go over the agreed time limit.

Also, keep in mind, this time has to come from somewhere, especially if you're part of a busy conference-presentation schedule or show. If you go over your time, then somebody else will lose some of theirs; whether it's taken from the next speaker or from your audience's lunch break, you're not making friends. Be respectful. Finish on time. Will anyone ever complain that your talk was too short? Wouldn't you rather not find out? Always leave your audience wanting more.

> Be respectful. Finish on time. Will anyone ever complain that your talk was too short? Wouldn't you rather not find out? Always leave your audience wanting more.

If you've crafted a memorable story, used the joke structures, and tested your material, then you're going to get some great laughs from the crowd. Make sure you allow them time to laugh. Also, remember your planning: "A tight five is much better than a sloppy fifteen." Aim to be consistently high (not that kind of high!), consistently funny, and consistently good. To do this, you're better off squeezing your time into a more compact time frame than allowing yourself to ramble around the clock.

If you are using a slide advancer, get one with a built-in vibrating alarm. If you're not, the best and often the most reliable way to keep on track is to ask for a signal light. This is where somebody in the audience, a friend or the organizer you have asked, will shine a light in your direction or give you a signal to let you know that your completion time is approaching. Some stages and conferences like TED have countdown clocks at the foot of the stage, but many still do not. It makes so much sense to have a clock on stage that it will become the accepted norm very quickly. Trust me, I know these things. Best prepare for it now.

Ideally, this signal will come with one or two minutes remaining, the exact amount of time necessary for your planned conclusion. The signal light can be something as simple as a smartphone, a laser pointer, or somebody waving a hand. Make sure you acknowledge that you saw the signal when preparing. Aim to finish a minute or more under at least. This will allow you time to incorporate elements we discussed in the last section like riffing or calling the room or reacting to something unexpected. Always plan to finish at least a minute under the imposed time limit.

Never End on Q&A

You finish your talk and the presenter takes back the mic. "Any questions for the speaker?" Awkward silence . . . "Anyone at all? Oh, you, sir, with your hand raised," the host says with a newfound blast of enthusiasm akin to a fisherman who has just hooked a big fish.

"I just yawned."

"Oh, sorry . . . anyone else? No? Nobody? Eh . . . right . . . okay then." The presenter slips away awkwardly amid confused, sporadic applause. This is how their video clip will end. True viral YouTube gold, crowd alive with energy and inspiration and multiple speakers' bureaus beating a path to your door. Not quite.

All too often speakers go out on a flat note because of this scenario. When you are expected to do a questions-and-answers session at the end of your talk, always save a summary slide to close with, ideally with three main takeaways. (There's that number again!) As you approach the end of your talk, say, "Okay I am going to take a few questions before I make my conclusion." This lets the audience know that you are not quite finished, keeps the Q&A shorter, and allows you to finish in a way that the audience knows it's over. When they know it's over they will applaud in unison. In leaving them with your main takeaways as a summary, you are also more likely to be remembered. Strong clapping in unison at the end will also mean better video.

Finally, make sure to soak up any applause. Stop talking and enjoy the moment. Only start speaking again when the applause begins to dwindle, and sometimes not even then. As Jerry told George in the classic 1998 *Seinfeld* episode, "The Burning": "Showmanship, George. When you hit that high note, you say goodnight and walk off."

Exercise: Timing and Delivery

Talk to the audience during your next public speaking engagement. Remember you are not there to give a theater performance. Engage the audience. They are more likely to pay attention if they think you may call on them at any moment.

Practice riffing and calling the room as you get more comfortable. Try and do this for at least one minute of your stage time allocation.

Practice making sure your talk comes in under the time limit. See what parts generate the biggest laughs and allow time for this and also riffing/calling the room. Ask for a signal light and get used to delivering a strong closing within the remaining time limit. One minute light, one minute closing; two minute light, two minute closing; et cetera. Know how long it takes you to make your closing remarks.

Run through your presentation in fast forward. Saying the words out loud as quickly as possible is a great technique to identify words and parts of your talk that may trip you up the day of your talk.

Break down each talk into components, record them, and know how long it takes to tell each (e.g., intro, pitch, additional details, story elements, numbers component, lessons, and main takeaways). Knowing the associated times for each part will help you craft the perfect performance. This also facilitates quickly making changes if your time slot is cut at the last minute, due to other speakers going over their time allocations. Trust me, it will happen sooner or later.

Actress, stand-up comic, philanthropist, and advocate for the disabled Maysoon Zayid delivers a hilarious and powerful TED talk called, "I Got 99 Problems . . . Palsy Is Just One." Watch it and note as many as you can of the comedic techniques she uses that have been outlined in this book.

Close the Book, but Not Fully—
Permanent Beta

*"The end of a melody is not its goal: but nonetheless,
had the melody not reached its end it would not have
reached its goal either."*

—Friedrich Nietzsche

Fortunately or unfortunately, winning The Moth story competition back in 2014 on that windswept summer-like evening in San Francisco meant I would take part in the series' biggest U.S. GrandSLAM final event, where ten smaller competition winners compete against each other in front of a sold-out, fourteen-hundred-person crowd. That was how I found myself on stage in such grandiose surroundings, about to lay an egg at the start of this book. The majority of the finalists were experienced stage performers, but the advantage the comedians had was clear: the top four scoring stories were also the four funniest. Three of the four were comedians. People *like* stories, but they tend to *love* funny stories. The three comedians' superior timing on joke lines, presence on stage, and delivery were all too evident. They had done this before. They knew where the laugh lines were and they knew to give the audience time to appreciate their every one. This "they" I speak of was now a group to which I temporarily belonged.

As always, my heartbeat raced many beats above normal while waiting my turn. My palms, as ever, sweated uncontrollably. The difference now, after over a year of experiments in public speaking, was that I fully knew this was normal (minus laying an egg for most of the regular population). I was about to do something extraordinary, something cool, and something most people would likely agree that my body should think twice about. With my story reminders locked up in my memory palace, I knew I would not go blank on stage. I had told the story before, in a comedy club, to a less engaged and more demanding audience, and it had worked well. I had also told it to my friends and family, and they always seemed to enjoy it. I knew where they would likely laugh, I knew my timing, and I would leave time for some impromptu comments so it would be fun for me to tell. It was my story, and I knew it better than anyone. A process once scarier than a shark, dentist, spider, and mother-in-law rolled into one was now manageable. My nerves were well shielded from the gazing, expectant eyes in the audience.

My story was about my less-traveled, conservative Irish mother making her way to San Francisco to nurse me back to health after I suffered a serious injury. San Francisco certainly rubbed off on her. She left wearing Lululemon yoga pants accompanied by a host of new, not-so-conservative habits. Two people connected by birth but separated by many years apart got closer, as highlighted by a text—a blue text, from her new iPhone—she sent after she left, saying, "David, I know we are mother and son but now it feels like we are friends."

My story was a big hit with the crowd, and with one storyteller left to take the stage, I was in first place, outscoring eight others. I waited to see if she would pull ahead of me, or if I'd stay in first place.

I didn't. The story told by the last Moth GrandSLAM participant that night was fantastic and so she left me, by a whisker, to claim the runner-up spot. I know . . . you were expecting a victory. To be honest, so was I. Where is the triumphant ending? Big, splashy victories are grand, and I would have loved one here, but I learned that it wasn't all a loss. In fact, in small losses there are often big victories, as you will find out in a few moments.

What happened to Ryan, the comedian who crushed his set, puked, snorted a pizza, and left the building in a blaze of glory? To be honest, I have no idea, but if I did, now would be the time to tell you.

Comedians will use what's known as a Bookend Technique. This is where they reference opening jokes and stories at the conclusion of their show. This gives their performance a feeling of completion and symmetry. They are far from alone in using this technique; the best writers, movie producers, and presenters all do the same thing. It can be found just about everywhere we look. It caters to our natural curiosity and search for completion.

The Bookend Technique can connect everything together—an essential element to a great talk or presentation. You have the chance to captivate an audience with your words and get them stuck in your story until its natural conclusion. There is no more powerful end to a story than when the audience knows it's over. They know where to applaud because the sequence of the story has delivered their cue. This is the essence of the Bookend Technique. Make sure you provide a natural conclusion to a well-glued sequence that keeps people stuck attentively until you are ready to close the book on your topic. Start with a story and close it off (or refer back to it) at the end. Business speakers and other presenters can utilize this approach by referring to their opening personal story in their closing remarks. This is essentially where you tie the start of your story to the end.

In Comedy Habit #1, we learned that crafting a good story means knowing where you want to take the audience. By writing the story with the punch line in mind, you will make it easy to tie the initial opening to your ultimate conclusion. Whatever closing technique you deploy, remember, if you get the chance, call on your inner comic and end your talk on an applause line that underscores a clear call to action.

This closing should be your highest-rated joke or story and should give a natural feeling of conclusion. Remember, it's not just about the comedy. Try to follow the examples of Martin Luther King, Steve Jobs, and Simon Sinek by incorporating a clear takeaway, be it a reinforced statement, a laugh line, or "one more thing."

I've told you why I was standing on stage at the Castro Theatre in front of fourteen hundred expectant pairs of eyes at the start of this book. Now let me tell you what happened with my friend Arash and why my loss that night was anything but.

Two stories intertwined.

A year's experiment in comedy left me with plenty of free time compared to the normal corporate routine. Every other week I drove Arash to his physical therapy center. It was one of the more inspirational places I have ever been. People fully focused on recovery and pushing their limits daily, for hours on end in pursuit of a dogged goal: to get back to the way they once were. So many of them had been abandoned by their insurance providers and given little chance of recovery, but they refused to give up. Many of them, like Arash, were reliant on fundraisers organized by friends to raise much-needed funds for this therapy. Along with Laura, one of Arash's childhood friends, we wondered how similar was Arash's predicament to that of other spinal cord injury (SCI) survivors? How many SCI survivors have been given little or no hope of recovery? How many like Arash are forced to pay out of pocket for necessities as fundamental as a wheelchair due to poor insurance? What are their experiences, and how do they deal with this life-altering condition?

To find this out, we spent the next few months conducting a survey to gather data. When the results were in, we recruited some friends well versed in the media to help get some of the more eye-opening findings out there.[38] To our shock and dismay, not one media outlet or journalist was interested. We knew this story had to be told, but numbers alone were not the way to do it.

After a nearly year of public speaking experiments and storytelling events, something dawned on me with the weight of someone who just walked 100 miles in the wrong direction: to tell the story of others, you must first tell your own. Numbers that attempted to outline a story did not give it enough life, color, or engagement to grab people's attention. Arash would have to tell his story before others would listen to him as a voice for others.

My real victory in all this came in using all I had learned to help Arash craft a talk. His first audience was to be three hundred CEOs, alongside top speakers like author and former chief evangelist of Apple, Guy Kawasaki. Arash started in the action by telling his own story in its shortest, most effective form, paused in all the right places, used the Rule of 3, built in callbacks, and left them with a bookended powerful message: life is about celebrating the small milestones that we often forget to acknowledge on the road to bigger goals—what he called "Little Big Steps," before showing a few of his own. He finished with an image of himself doing something doctors told him he would not be able to do: standing for a few minutes on his own two feet, temporarily free from his so-hated wheelchair, atop an old wooden pier on the shores of deep blue Lake Tahoe, to propose eye to eye to his beautiful girlfriend. Unfortunately, she said, no . . . just kidding, she of course said yes. "Little Big Steps," he reminded them, before he said, "Thank you," leaving them to stand and applaud for the next twenty seconds.

His second talk got a mention in *Forbes* for the memory palace techniques he used, which I'd passed on from my comedian friend Richard Sarvate's animated sushi chefs and sombrero-wearing Krishna.[39] Now very much a motivational speaker by circumstance, Arash's third talk was set to be even more high level.

Why am I telling you all this? "It's not relevant to funny public speaking," I hear you say. And you are right, in part. But not every story has to be funny. Often a story alone in its most naked, personal, impassioned form is plenty to move mountains and alter people's lives. To you, the teller, you are just telling a story . . . like I was on that hardwood stage in such grand surroundings to fourteen hundred people. But to the listeners, something in that shared experience or moment of temporary magic—which can make the most distant of circumstances seem tailor fit to them—can alter the course of their lives. You may not remember all fourteen hundred people, but if you do a good job and deliver your talk using many of the techniques comedians know only too well, whether it's four or fourteen hundred people, they will remember you.

Too serious a topic for humor?

Arash's story is obviously a serious and hard-hitting one, and a topic you may assume is not forthcoming to humor. Quite the opposite can be true, as was the case with fellow Irishman Mark Pollock. Addressing the audience at TEDx Hollywood, he rolled out onto the stage in his wheelchair and opened with the following: "Ladies and gentlemen, I have got problems. I'm paralyzed. I'm blind. I'm bald. I'm from Northern Ireland. I've got problems. There is no doubt about that. I suspect some of you do also." Mark immediately took something so severe, tragic, and unrelatable to many and made it suddenly very relatable. In situations where there is high tension, laughter often brings great relief. Maysoon Zayid uses a similar structure to great effect in her TED talk. Talking about her cerebral palsy, she says, "I got 99 problems and palsy is just one. If there was an oppression Olympics I would win the gold medal. I'm Palestinian, Muslim, I'm female, I'm disabled and . . . I live in New Jersey." At San Francisco's historic Geary Theater, writer, photographer, and adventurer Anya Rymer told over one thousand people at a Moth Mainstage event about her turbulent battles with AIDS. "I had at one point only eight T cells left," she said. "I called them the Brady Bunch."

A Real Victory

A week after the storytelling final, a high-profile TEDx conference producer who saw my story contacted me and asked if I would like to speak at their next event. As fate would have it, I had a friend I could recommend in my place that I knew would be perfect. One who had a true inspirational story just waiting to be told. I sent the producer the link to Arash's first talk and he booked him immediately in my place. On a blustery early fall evening in Marin County, California, Arash told his story to more than six hundred people at a sold-out TEDx event. He was the final speaker, and I watched eagerly from backstage as the audience again stood to applaud, this time for nearly fifty seconds, when he reminded them of the importance of "Little Big Steps" before standing to show a few of his own.

Stories are always said to be powerful, but I learned something else that night: to tell the story of others, you will likely need to tell yours first. Nobody is more qualified to tell it than you, and you never know what will happen when you do. Once you've closed the book on your story like Arash did, say, "Thank you." Nothing more. "You have been wonderful," "Thanks for having me," "Great to be here," "That's my time," are all unnecessary. (You can watch Arash's talk here: http://www.tedxmarin.org/2015-speakers/arash-bayatmakou/. You can listen to my story by going to **http://www.7comedyhabits.com/book-resources** and also get a breakdown of the storytelling and comedic techniques mentioned in this book that I used to craft it.)

Now that we've just about closed the book on our story, we're going to move on to a process of evaluation.

Watch Your Words Play

Professional comedians will continuously evaluate every performance, seeking to move from Good to Very Good to Excellent, and so should you. They keep practicing even when they're already performing at a very high level, just like Jerry Seinfeld. Never do they say, "That's it, I'm awesome, no point or need to prepare anymore." They're always seeking to develop and improve. They need to be pleased, but never satisfied, with every performance. The idea of being in Permanent Beta, that there's always room for improvement, is a perspective that will set you up for success as a speaker.

It's estimated that new comedians put together between five and eight new minutes of really strong material in their first year. When we say really strong material, we mean consistently high laughs all the time. Again, here, we need only a fraction of that. For our purposes, a couple of key jokes and consistently funny stories that can be inserted into our presentations is more than enough.

The value of testing.

Thomas Edison evaluated 6,000 plants before deciding to use bamboo for the filament in his exciting new invention, the electric light bulb. The lesson here? *You need to test!*

To do this, we're going to continuously evaluate every performance with this scoring system taken from the book *The Comedy Bible* by Judy Carter. Using this system, we'll be evaluating each bit based on laughs per minute. We'll award:

- 5 points for every time everybody laughs out loud and applauds
- 4 points when there's laughter and one or two claps
- 3 points when there's laughter but no applause
- 2 points when there's medium laughs
- 1 point for very few laughs

Using this system, we'll be able to eliminate personal bias (i.e., jokes or stories that we like to tell, but did not generate a favorable reaction every time). Our presentation material is always going to be a work in progress that can be improved, and we want to use this scoring system to highlight those jokes that work every time regardless of the audience we use them with.

When I applied this to my own stories, it made a huge difference. Patterns quickly emerged as stories I thought worked well were outscored by bits I was not as attached to. The numbers don't lie.

Sammy Obeid is the first comedian to ever perform for 1,000 days (1,001 nights) consecutively, which he completed in September 2013, capping off his progression with an appearance on Conan (see https://www.youtube.com/watch?v=W2m7THG44tM). I was lucky enough to share the stage with him at Cobb's Comedy Club in San Francisco recently. Sammy has long been a driven, goal-oriented perfectionist. He earned a 3.9 grade point average at the University of California, Berkeley, majoring in applied mathematics and business administration, before trying comedy, which he approached with the same rigor.

"Jokes can be very systematic," Sammy said. "What is the right word that fits in this blank to make this equation work?" Similar to Judy's system, as outlined above, Sammy rates jokes from D to A+. "B's can one day turn to A's, which can turn to A+'s. I've seen it happen many times. Some of my best bits have started off as a B, and then I added, trimmed, and structured and now they are at A+. My belief actually, is that any B can be an A if you find a way. Yeah, that rhymes for a reason. Work out your B's, but make sure you choose a show that's low pressure, in front of a crowd that isn't too big or is at least very merciful. And have backup plans. Intersperse with A's. I've been doing this for so long, so I take greater risks. I'll do C's interspersed with B's, and then if I'm really losing them, throw in the A's. How do you know if a joke is a B or an A or a C? It depends on your standards. For me, A's kill most of the time. B's get some laughs, but don't really kill. C's seem funny, but don't really get that many laughs. D's suck."

What we see as funny in life is often tried and tested. This includes movies, advertisements, and comedy shows. They tend to leave little to chance and borrow a lot from structure and testing. With this in mind, we need to review our jokes and stories and allocate the relevant score to each. Take this from every performance, not just one night. We want to add up the total and divide by the total minutes on stage. This will give us a laughs per minute (LPM) score. For reference, 12–20 LPM is good for any professional comedian; 9–12 means you would be ready to get paid as a comedian but need to shorten your setups. And by shortening your setup, we mean cut out the amount of words it takes to get to the punch line ("Brevity Is Levity"). Remember, this system was designed for comedians performing in comedy venues where everybody is trying to be funny. A score of 4–9 means you will be very funny presenting in a business context, and anything over zero means you will be funnier than most other business speakers, who for the most part are not funny!

If we apply this scoring system to Ken Robinson's talk, the most viewed on TED at the time of writing, we get (give or take a few for personal opinion) nearly 7 LPM—enough to rival an up-and-coming comedian. If we take a weighted score away from how much they laugh and just record how many times they laughed as a group we get (give or take a few for personal bad math) approximately 2.8 laughs per minute. For comparison, when the same system was reported in *Forbes* magazine as applied by Lovefilm, the London-based video streaming service, these were the top funniest movies of all time.[40] Importantly, this does not take into account how big the laughs were—just the frequency.

Rank	Title	Laughs per Minute
1	*Airplane!*	3
2	*The Hangover*	2.4
3	*Naked Gun: From the Files of Police Squad!*	2.3
4	*Superbad*	1.9
5	*Borat*	1.7
6	*Anchorman: The Legend of Ron Burgundy*	1.6
7	*American Pie*	1.5
8	*Bridesmaids*	1.4
9	*Shaun of the Dead*	1.3
10	*Monty Python's Life of Brian*	1.2

On a laughs-per-minute basis, Ken is funnier than *The Hangover* and a hell of a lot more informative! Combine his high amount of laugher with passion and insightful, inspirational information and we have the ingredients of something really powerful. Is it any wonder we all love it? And he is not alone:

The 10 most popular general TED Talks as of this writing (not the top 10 funniest, importantly):

Rank	Title	Laughs per Minute
1	Ken Robinson: Do schools kill creativity?	2.8
2	Amy Cuddy: Your body language shapes who you are	0.9
3	Simon Sinek: How great leaders inspire action	0.27
4	Brené Brown: The power of vulnerability	2.1
5	Jill Bolte Taylor: My stroke of insight	1.1
6	Mary Roach: 10 things you didn't know about orgasm	3.4
7	Tony Robbins: Why we do what we do	1.3
8	Dan Pink: The puzzle of motivation	0.82
9	Pranav Mistry: The thrilling potential of Sixth Sense technology	0.44
10	David Gallo: Underwater astonishments	1.1
(12)	Shawn Achor: The happy secret to better work (My own personal favorite)	2.9

Mary Roach's talk about female orgasm generated more laughs per minute than the funniest movie ever made. (Note for the men on this one: if you are ever asked if you are familiar with Roach's talk while in female company, and you are not, at least nod enthusiastically and fake it. Maybe even add some additional vocal appreciation.) The power of vulnerability delivered by a researcher generated more laughs per minute than all but three of the world's funniest movies. *Body Language* with Amy Cuddy is not far off *Life of Brian*, a timeless 1979 British comedy film starring and written by a whole comedy group. Yes, these numbers are loose and are meant to be tongue in cheek, don't factor in an allowance for the varied running times, don't allow for the level of laughter generated (and I am sure the movies generate bigger, more laugh-out-loud lines), but the underlying point is there for all to see. Top TED speakers are using humor and some extremely well.

Our new top 5 (where Hollywood meets TED):

Rank	Title	Laughs per Minute
1	Mary Roach: 10 things you didn't know about orgasm	3.4
2	*Airplane!*: What crazy people do on a plane	3
3	Shawn Achor: The happy secret to better work	2.9
4	Ken Robinson: Do schools kill creativity?	2.8
5	*The Hangover*: How drunk guys do wacky stuff	2.4

Expect *TED the Movie: Information for an ADD Nation*, featuring a host of star speakers. Coming soon to a theater near you!

Most business speakers are completely boring, so by incorporating even a few laughs and some personal stories, your presentation will stand out from the crowd like many of the best TED talks do. High laugh-per-minute accounts will translate into an entertaining and engaging presentation.

By looking through multiple public speaking performances, you will be able to quickly identify the jokes and stories and patterns that work every time regardless of the venue. The goal is to look at jokes that score 3 (B), 4 (A), and 5 (A+) consistently. The other ones we're going to leave to one side. If your joke is scoring a 3, for example, you need to rework it a bit. There's something funny in there, but you haven't quite developed it to its maximum efficiency yet. If something is scoring 4 and 5, you have a really great joke that you can take out and incorporate into a presentation, knowing it will get a great response almost every time. Get systematic. The best speakers, like Ken Robinson, Mary Roach, and Sammy Obeid, always are.

Remember, continuously evaluate as you practice and perform, since there's always room for improvement. This is Permanent Beta. Close the book on your story but never fully on your performance.

And if you happen to see a man along the way fitting Ryan's description, do drop me a note.

Exercise: Evaluation and Permanent Beta

Watch this TED talk: "Shawn Achor: The Happy Secret to Better Work." It is one of my favorites and, like Ken Robinson's, a great example of the power of a well-crafted story and laugh lines. Apply the scoring system to it to get a feel for the process and calculate the laughs per minute. Note his opening story, which accounts for more than 20 percent of his overall talk time.

Work back through your own evaluated joke scores. This is where we aim to link what worked in practice with what you hope to present. Whether you were practicing on friends, family, colleagues, comedy clubs, or conferences, give it a score.

List each public speaking performance in a series of columns side-by-side, filling in each joke/story you told and its allocated score.

Identify which parts led to the best reactions. This also works well for identifying interest levels. Which parts led to confused looks or questions, or had people on the edge of their seats.

Find the ones that get the highest ratings consistently.

Also note any jokes/stories that seem to work well in a certain order or where you're able to incorporate callbacks successfully.

Highlight jokes that rate 3, 4, or 5 in busy venues or that always get at least some laughs out of a tough audience. The audience ideally should be real by this point, but if you're not quite stage ready yet, don't worry. You can use this system to note reactions from friends, colleagues, and strangers who hear your stories.

You will likely find that your highest-rated material follows the joke structure and often also has the fewest words.

Test different-order opening and closing variations of these jokes.

Try and work these lines into your stories and overall presentations where possible.

Look to extract your most engaging stories, best opening lines, and best closing jokes.

Conclusion

*"People want a thrill, people want a spectacle, and
people love to be entertained."*
—Paul Stanley

Modern-day speakers and presenters face competition like never before. Distractions, ringtones, and vibrations are the hallmark of our cultural attention deficit. Presenters are expected to be entertainers. Those who are do much better. Those who grab attention are more likely to hold it. Top speakers are already using one of the most powerful tools available to mankind to do this—laughter. Nothing will put you more at ease when speaking publicly than knowing you can make an audience laugh at a point of your choosing—better still, when doing just that will make you a standout.

Too many speakers present information in a boring manner. Choose not to. Never do what everyone else is doing. Find the few most successful people and do what they are doing differently. My argument in this book is that the most successful speakers are using humor, storytelling, and improv techniques, even if many are unaware of it. This awareness could save you precious time when focusing on 20 percent of the inputs that generate 80 percent of the results.

James Altucher says that 90 percent of success is showing up, so take the first step and get started.[41] Have fun, play, and be creative. If you're having fun, others will, too.

Born on a comedy stage, laugh lines are equally at home on a TED stage. I hope you get to share yours, however big or small your goals. If, like me, you're afraid of public speaking, don't worry—the process will become manageable. With increased stage time comes higher levels of comfort. Make it a habit and you'll make Shakin' Stevens disappear.

The whole audience won't always like what you say. Wise words from Gabrielle Reece, former professional volleyball player, *Sports Illustrated* model, and wife of Surf God Laird Hamilton, ring very true here. When asked how she deals with the pressures of her career, she said, "In life, you will always have 30 percent of people who love you, 30 percent who hate you, and 30 percent who couldn't care less."[42] Who knows what happened to the other 10 percent, but the point is still very true. Don't worry about trying to please everyone. You don't need all of the audience on your side to be a good speaker; 30 percent is plenty. Laughter is contagious. You might find it starts to spread quickly if you give it time. Ten percent of life is what happens to you, while 90 percent is what you make happen. Make a point of adding humor.

The Comedy for a Spinal Cause fundraiser for Arash that got me into all this in the first place went so well that it's now an ongoing quarterly event bringing together top comedians and local communities with the goal of raising funds and awareness to assist incredible individuals on their road to recovering from spinal cord injury.[43] Arash is pretty close to permanently getting back on his feet despite being told he would never walk again. At the time of writing, we have helped raise more than $34,000 for people with spinal cord injuries—just a drop in the ocean of what is needed, but enough to make a difference. And I host it a lot less reluctantly now. Why was I not my usual bag of nerves when it comes to hosting the event? Because I had prepared, practiced, and put in the stage time. I put together a tried-and-tested collection of stories I knew would make people laugh by using the techniques I have outlined in this book. You will, too. And you will be able to do it quickly.

Along the way, I met a host of businesspeople struggling to create good content, whether it was verbal, written, or in marketing materials. There is no magic bullet for viral content, but it was obvious the world of business also had strayed from the building blocks of spreadable engaging content, story, and humor.

Born to solve this problem and bridge the gap between business and comedy, I founded FunnyBizz Conferences (http://funnybizz.co/funnybizz-conference). All our speakers come from the world of business, TED, and comedy and are always funny. They often have a sneaky background in stand-up, improv, storytelling, or a deep love of humor. Talks are limited to short periods, and we have no keynote speakers. Just like a stand-up set, we seek to start strong and finish even stronger. There is always a clock on stage and speakers never run it (well, for the most part; old habits die hard). The conferences are pretty cool and like none I have ever been to before. I guess that was the point: see what everyone else is doing and don't do it. Unsolicited testimonials like this one make me think others agree, and I feel privileged to be involved:

"Most conferences are like swimming in a nice comfy bowl of familiar oatmeal. This one was more like putting on a cape and diving off a building. FunnyBizz delivered more than take-aways and actionable ideas. FunnyBizz delivered a

mode-changing experience right into my brain. If you can only go to one conference a year, it should be this one."

Just like with the charity fundraiser, I am now fully confident in my ability to host a great conference without the crippling fear of failure that once turned me into a puddle of jelly, even when things go wrong and the shit nearly—and very literally—hit the fan.

At a recent event in New York City, we temporarily ran out of toilet paper. This is not uncommon at big events where the venue provides the janitorial support stuff. They can only do so much, so quickly. Well, on this occasion they needed to go *más rápido* because we had just fed the crowd a delicious Mexican buffet for lunch and were just about to give them a bunch of free alcohol. Not exactly a winning combination.

What did we do? Just like comedians do, just like the best speakers do, and just like Biz Stone did at Twitter, we called attention to the obvious and acknowledged the likely feelings of the audience to defuse the situation: *"Guys, sincere apologies. We are a conference on humor and maybe we went too far. Feeding you Mexican food, giving you free alcohol, and hiding the toilet paper. Not funny, guys. Not funny at all."* (Note the Rule of 3 here as well as the joke structure: setup—punch line—tagline.) The incident was addressed in a positive way, in the moment, and with a humorous nature that meant it was the last we heard of it.

As I write this, I am at the Kansas City Irish Fest alongside many of Ireland's top musicians and 90,000 attendees over the long Labor Day weekend. I just spoke to a sold-out crowd of 300 at the Kansas City Library, performed stand-up comedy to a packed-to-the-rafters theater beside one of Ireland's top comedians, did an interview for National Public Radio, was a panelist on a TV show's pilot recording, sat in hallway musical jam sessions until the wee hours of the morning, and overall got a short glimpse into the rock star lifestyle—the highlight of which was watching a sweat-laden singer in midday heat use the emergency phone from the fancy rooftop hotel pool to inform the concerned operator that he needed a beer delivered poolside immediately, because he was dying . . . of thirst.

How all this came to be I am not certain—but I do know it was a sequence of events I began with the aim of overcoming a fear. I may or may not keep doing comedy and storytelling nights. Like most people, I find the demands of business all too often get in the way of fun, but now, like you, I have a way of often combining the two. Funny enough, speaking with the crowd assembled at the Kansas City Library felt much better than performing stand-up comedy in the theater. Why? Because I was not just making them laugh but giving them actionable learning points, wrapped in a story that I felt had the potential to make a long-lasting difference in not only their lives but also those of many others.

Modern-day public speaking forces you to become a performer, and as such your happiness will often be determined by the happiness of those for whom you perform. Make sure it's a mutual exchange of happiness and learning—and of course, where you can, rock it.

> " Modern-day public speaking forces you to become a performer, and as such your happiness will often be determined by the happiness of those for whom you perform. "

Just like my home in California at the time of writing, we are in the midst of a drought. It is, however, a different kind of drought I refer to: a laughter drought. Babies laugh, on average, 300 times a day; people over thirty-five years old, *only fifteen*! Safe to say anyone who can bring back some of these lost laughter moments can quickly affirm themselves as a hero. Your newfound elevated status may be limited to your time on stage. However, when combined with some real information and concrete learning points, and crafted amid a memorable and humorous story, you may find your star burns brighter for longer. I truly hope it does. Let us rid the world of boring content one presentation at a time! The world is waiting for your funny stories. Only you are qualified to tell them, and you never know what may happen when you do.

Where you can, *add comedy*. We all need more of it.

7 Comedy Habits

Start with a Story

Add Humor - Find the Funny

Write Funny

Rehearsed Spontaneity

Delivery - Start Strong,
Finish Stronger

Control the Audience

Close The Book, But Not Fully. Permanent Beta

Further Material

Six months after The Moth storytelling final at the Castro Theatre, I bumped into the lady who left me to take second place that night. On quizzing her about what training she had to beat out three comedians that night, she revealed that one book she came across had been helpful and proceeded to show me the notes she had made on her smartphone. It listed seven comedy habits and a host of words that looked all too familiar. They were taken from an earlier version of the book you are now reading. The irony was not lost on me as I grinned from cheek to cheek.

Outside The Moth I did all my comedy and storytelling nights under various stage names, most commonly "Irish Dave"—a name that to the best of my knowledge has only been used by one other comedian, the much-beloved and hugely successful Dave Allen, who passed away in 2005. He was born ironically in Firhouse, the same neighborhood in Dublin I grew up in—a fact I only discovered several months into my journey.

I didn't give the rights to any of my footage to anyone, as the goal of this experiment was never then, nor is now, to become a famous comedian, mildly famous comedian, or even a comedian at all. It was to overcome a fear. As such, the only place (hopefully!) you can find video links to my own examples, is via the link below. I would like to share my videos only with you, the reader, as you now know my story. I would greatly appreciate if you didn't share them online with anyone else. Here you can also find most of the examples described, additional book resources, supporting images, and further reading: **7comedyhabits.com/book-resources**.

Not all items and examples made this book. It is a short read, and I wanted to keep it so. Trust me, being Irish, I had plenty more words in me but had to remind myself that brevity is levity.

Books, especially from new authors like myself, live or die by reviews. If you enjoyed this one, it would be hugely appreciated if you could take thirty seconds and leave one, saying something as deep as, "Book good, me likey." Feel free to get more creative, profound, or even (now that you know how) funny! Thanks a million for taking the time to read my book. Honestly, I thought I had more chance of getting myself pregnant than ever writing one, so I am truly humbled that you did.

Finally, to all those who want to add humor and help rid the world of boring content: thanks for reading! Go forth and multiply. The world needs more fine specimens like you. If you need help along the way, ask a comedian. They are the true masters.

Tipliography

About now most books have a bibliography that's none too exciting.
Rather than follow suit with what's normal, here I have summarized
many of the tips in this book and added some more from many of the
ten-thousand-hour comedians I met over the course of my experiment or drew wisdom from along the way. The following are eighty
tips that should help you brush up on your funny before your next
public speaking gig.

1 Draw Upon Your Own Real-Life Experiences
"The safest humor involves personal stories, because they are guaranteed to be original and unheard, they can be practiced and perfected, and they are highly personalized to your style," says Alan
Weiss.

2 Speak about What You Like
Tell the stories that you already tell around your colleagues, friends,
and family. Work to build them into your talk. If you don't like what
you are talking about, nobody else will either. Complete this sentence: (Your Name here) is always talking about . . .

3 Find the Key Point to Each Story
Where is the funny anecdote, interesting bit of knowledge, or the
entertaining part? Work to cut out unnecessary words and re-tell the
best stories using the following rule of thumb: Three lines with no
funny are too much.

Get to the Funny Fast

U.K. comedian Jimmy Carr says, "Writing comedy isn't really about writing; it's more about editing. It's about what you don't say. What are the fewest words I can get down here in order to get to the funny bit?"

Think Fails and Firsts

"So many people ask me for help creating a funnier speech," says Darren LaCroix. "They want to know where to 'find funny.' I suggest starting by looking in the mirror! Start by looking at your fails and your firsts. The first time you did something wrong. Audiences love the humility and openness."

Play with Your Pain

"To truly laugh, you must be able to take your pain and play with it," Charlie Chaplin said. While he likely didn't mean customer pain points, the same wisdom applies.

Listen and Repeat

"Many funny things are said and done in your presences that are wholly original and can be used as a humorous illustration in your stories or speech," says Pat Hazell. "I overheard my kids arguing during a candy exchange after Halloween that was a wonderful message about value in negotiations. My oldest son Tucker said, 'I hate dark chocolate!' To which his brother responded, 'It's still candy, you got to respect that.' I use the dialogue verbatim because it is so pure and to the point."

Start a Funny Story File

As you begin to take notes and observe the world around you while looking for humor, you'll find it gives you plenty of opportunities to find it. Every time you think of something funny or you have an observation or something that you think will be useful, make sure you write it down. If you have a smartphone, use your notes section or an app like Evernote. You'll be surprised just how quickly you forget these thoughts.

Use the Rule of 3

This rule is a basic structure for jokes and ideas that capitalizes on the way we process information. We have become proficient at pattern recognition by necessity. Three is the smallest number of elements required to create a pattern. This combination of pattern and brevity results in memorable content.

Feed Your Stories into the Joke Structure

Note the Rule of 3:

1. Introduction/Setup: Introduce your topic remembering, "Brevity is levity." No more than three lines before the funny.
2. Punch Line: Key funny part to your story. Try and keep anticipation to the end if possible. Often the best jokes are when the key funny part only becomes apparent with the very last word.
3. Taglines (optional): Additional jokes/comments that build on the initial joke.

Take the Train Off Track

The punch line shatters the intentionally built-up interest and expectation. According to corporate humorist John Kinde, "A funny line is sometimes said to be like a train wreck. You know where the train (your train of thought) has been, you think you know where it's going, but then you're surprised when it goes off track."

Jokes Are: 1, 2 . . . 4!

"They look like they're about to establish a pattern but then break it just when it's about to become one," says Rajiv Satyal. "In this example, you think I'm counting but, when you hear '4,' you realize I was doubling the numbers. It makes sense in retrospect. (But they're not 1, 2 . . . 7! That would just be random.) Jokes work due to the element of surprise. Too many business presentations are stuff people already know (1, 2 . . . 3!) or stuff people don't know what to do with (1, 2 . . . 7!). Give 'em something both memorable and fun."

13 Get a Quick Laugh

There is always a tension in the room as the audience tries to figure out a little bit about you and decides if they want to listen to you. Getting a quick laugh can be a great way to lighten the mood.

14 Develop an Opening Line

As any 100-meter sprinter knows, it's much harder to win if you get off to a weak start. The first thirty seconds of your presentation can set the tone for the rest of your talk as easily as the sprinter's time off the block. Rehearse this thirty seconds the most.

15 Acknowledge the Obvious

If you're visibly nervous, have a fresh stain on your shirt, or if there's anything unusual about you physically—anything that the audience might fixate on at the start—now is the time to address it, get a laugh, and move on so the audience can focus. Acknowledging the obvious is known in comedy as "calling the room." It means vocalizing exactly what's going on in the room or what people are likely thinking.

16 Think Fun Over Funny

"Making people laugh is only one type of humor; getting them to smile is another," says Andrew Tarvin. "When starting out, focus on making things fun as opposed to making things funny."

17 Take a Bar Exam

Unlike conference rooms, bars are friendly, social places. People expect stories told there to be succinct and entertaining. That's why IDEO marketing lead and Mortified co-producer Annette Ferrara tells designers to "take a bar exam." Go to a bar with a colleague—or imagine you're in one—and tell your story using only napkin drawings as your visuals. Have your friend repeat back your story to see what's sticking and what's not. Refine and repeat.

"A sense of humor is an attitude in how you approach your work and life. It is a skill that can be developed."
–Jeanne Robertson

18 Use Tension

"There has to be tension for a punch line to land," says Zahra Noorbakhsh. "Tension sets up the desire to see a problem—however big or small—get resolved. If you can identify what is making your audience restless, anxious, or uncomfortable, you can work backward to find the joke that chills them out."

19 Use the Art of Misdirection

"The beautiful thing about a business presentation versus stand-up comedy is that the presentation audience can be misled into a funny line much easier," says Cody Woods. "Due to the many boring presentations they have been subjected to, they are suspecting it less. Use this to your advantage."

20 Put the Word the Joke Hinges On at the End of the Sentence

"For example, if the fact it's a cat is the surprise or twist, don't say, 'There was a cat in the box' Say, 'In that box was a cat.' That way you're not still talking when they're meant to be laughing," says Matt Kirshen.

21 Use Metaphors and Analogies Combined with Hyperbole (Exaggeration)

"Figure out the pattern of something you're criticizing, and then choose a metaphor that makes that look ridiculous," says Brian Carter. "For example, I might teach that trying to do organic social marketing without ads, maybe hoping for it to go viral, is like trying to drive a car that only other people can fill up with gas when they feel like it and hoping they will. Exaggerating anything makes it funnier. So I could exaggerate the previous example and say that it's like the *Star Trek* Enterprise trying to fly to a new star system without any dilithium crystals and hoping that some Klingons show up and give them some. Now, I just made those up and they're probably horrible, but that illustrates the process (Trekkies get it)."

"Aim for charming and enjoyable instead of hilarious."
–Doug Kessler

22 Paint a Picture for Others to See

"Comedy is in the details, but you don't want to overdo it," says Reggie Steele. "Just enough to set the scene. Talk to people as if you're talking to a blind person or you're doing something for the radio. Details matter."

23 Use Current Media References Where Possible

Creating material that relates to topics that are current in the mind of those in our audience is another easy way to get a laugh. Nighttime television hosts like John Oliver, Stephen Colbert, and Jimmy Fallon are masters of this, and their popularity heightens the chance that your crowd already will be familiar with poking fun at fresh topics.

24 Tell a Joke

If people laugh, a joke has already added value. "It helps if it segues into a point. But it doesn't have to," says Rajiv Satyal. One of his favorites that's both hilarious and yet clean enough for a corporate presentation: A guy joins a monastery and takes a vow of silence. He's allowed to say two words every seven years. After the first seven years, the elders bring him in and ask for his two words. He says, "Cold floors." They nod and send him away. Seven more years pass. They bring him back in and ask for his two words. He clears his throat. "Bad food," he says. They nod and send him away. Seven more years pass. They bring him in for his two words. He goes, "I quit." One of the elders looks at him and says, "That's not surprising. You've done nothing but complain since you got here."

"I've never had that joke miss in any context," says Satyal. And it's easy to tie it into something going on at a company, such as a reorg. (Every place is always doing a reorg.)

25 Start Strong and Finish Even Stronger

Start with your second-best part. Leave the best until last.

"To truly laugh, you must be able to take your pain,
and play with it."
—Charlie Chaplin

26 Run Through Your Presentation in Fast Forward

Saying the words out loud as quickly as possible is a great technique to identify words and parts of your talk that may trip you up the day of your talk.

27 Don't Bring Visible Notes Onstage with You

Podiums are becoming a thing of the past as most organizers realize they create a barrier between the speaker and audience, so sooner or later you'll have nowhere to put notes. It's best not to rely on them at all, but if you must have something, be sneaky about it. Write a few notes on a water bottle label or a napkin. Notes should stay in your back pocket throughout. If you don't have a back pocket, get creative. Visible notes show the audience that you're not fully prepared and also force you to break flow and eye contact.

28 Avoid Going Blank Onstage

Use the "memory palace" memorization technique. "To do this, it is useful to have the image interact with the environment," Richard Sarvate says. "For my sushi joke, I picture a sushi chef. If I put him in the elevator in the lobby of my apartment, I picture him mashing the buttons on the elevator in frustration. Now that he is interacting with the environment, it's a lot easier to visualize and recall. It's useful to make the image bizarre in order to make it more memorable. For my Mexican-Indian joke, I picture Krishna wearing a sombrero. A ridiculous image, which is almost tougher to forget."

29 Close Your Wardrobe

President Obama, Albert Einstein, and Steve Jobs are all known as proponents for the ease of selecting the same items for all public appearances. Having standard speaking attire means one less thing you have to worry about. It also makes your video reel clips easier to stitch together.

30 Wear Dark, Sweat-Proof Clothing

Presenting in front of an audience takes energy and focus, which means you will perspire. Instead of feeling uncomfortable with visible sweat stains, dress for success. Make sure your presentation wardrobe includes fabrics like 100 percent cotton, linen, lightweight merino wool, jersey, chambray, rayon, silk or moisture wick fabric.

31 Don't Wait to Work the Room

Try and introduce yourself to as many people in the room as possible before you start to speak. It helps break down that initial barrier that a stage can create. Don't wait until you have already addressed the audience to start working the room.

32 Avoid Stage Fright

This is your body's way of telling you that it is ready. The thought of negative consequences triggers glands to secrete the hormone ACTH. This hormone results in the release of adrenaline into your blood and that's what causes these uncomfortable feelings. This is essentially your body's most alert and heightened state. It means you're ready. You want to focus on embracing this feeling. When you feel it, be happy. It means your body is in its peak condition to face a challenging or worrying situation.

33 No Drinking or Other Substances Prior to Your Talk

You want to fully embrace your heightened state of alertness.

34 Watch the Three Speakers before You

This allows you to build on their success and call back to their jokes. It also makes you are aware of any overlapping examples and helps avoid unnecessary repeats.

35 Stretch First

Just before you go on stage, put your hands above your head in a full stretch. This will help calm your nerves.

"Stories are the creative conversion of life itself into a more powerful, clearer, more meaningful experience. They are the currency of human contact."
–Robert McKee

36 Get Your Intro Right

Don't leave your introduction to chance. Always supply one in advance. Many hosts or emcees try to improvise humorous interludes themselves. Don't let their laughs be at your expense. The only time the introduction should ever mention your name is at the very end. This is the audience's cue to applaud for you.

37 Let the Host Sell You

Have the host list your achievements, why you are qualified to be there, and why the audience should listen to you, so you don't have to. This allows you to start with a story rather than a chronological self-promotional ordering of your achievements, however big or small.

38 Get Onstage Fast

As soon as the host introduces you (hopefully with a round of applause), quickly make your way onto the stage. You should be in position to commence speaking as soon as the applause dwindles. If, for any reason, you need to set up or adjust some items at this point in time, it's a great moment to ask the audience for a round of applause for your host or previous speaker.

39 If the Energy Is Down, Bring It Up

"If the host didn't introduce you with a strong round of applause, this is a good time for you to ask the audience to offer a round of applause," says Sarah Cooper. "Feel free to ask for a round of applause for the presenter, the host, some of the presenters before you, the sponsor or organizers of the event, and even one for the audience themselves (even though they think they're clapping for themselves, it still feels like they're clapping for you)." Applause also follows the Rule of 3. It gets the audience into the habit of applauding and laughing.

"As a creator, it's your job to make an audience as
excited and fascinated about a subject as you are, and
real life tends to do that."
–Ricky Gervais

40 Cut the Fluff

Outside asking for applause if it is needed, start your talk in the action. Don't say, "I am happy to be here," "Great to be here," "It's my first time in this city," "There are so many of you," "Wow, what a great day," et cetera. Get to it.

41 Smile and Make Eye Contact

Connect with as many people as you can in the front rows for the duration of the first thirty seconds and as much as you can throughout the rest of your talk. This helps you to engage as many members of the audience as you can on a personal level. If you look like you're enjoying it and you look happy, chances are other people will start to as well.

42 Speak Up, Not "Ah," "Eh," "But"

It sounds straightforward enough, but make sure you speak loud enough for people to hear you. You need to reach everybody in the room. The added benefit is that by speaking at little as 20 percent louder than normal, you will reduce the amount of filler words ("ah," "eh," "but") you tend to use. It's hard to say "eh" or "em" with this higher-than-normal tone. This feels strange to do but sounds perfectly normal to your audience.

43 Don't Eat the Microphone

This should fall under the "instinct" category, but you can't be sure with people these days. Don't underestimate what your nerves might drive you to do. New presenters tend to keep it a little bit too close to their mouth. Keep it a good distance away from your mouth; ideally, keep it down by your chin. If you are really nervous, leave the mic in the stand until you get a few early laughs and feel more confident. Then once the nerves have calmed, move the stand out of the way.

44 Trust Yourself and Your Material

If you look like you know what you're doing, people will believe it and that confidence is infectious. Remember, people are fundamentally good at heart. Nobody wants to see a speaker or performer doing badly. They want to see you succeed. Give them reason to think you will.

45 Don't Spray Your Words

Make eye contact with a friendly face in the audience and hold for three seconds at a time. (Any longer gets creepy fast!) Only move between faces at pause points in your talk—at a new sentence, sentence break, or pause point. Avoid standing there spraying your words around the audience. This will give you better camera footage every time.

46 Speak Instead of Preach

Be conversational on stage and avoid preaching. This relaxes the audience and makes it seem more of a spontaneous discussion.

47 Add Attitude

Use words like *weird*, *amazing*, *scary*, *hard*, *stupid*, *crazy*, or *nuts*. Try to incorporate these words into your opening setup or statement. This will help people focus on you and pay attention quickly. If you want people to be passionate about your topic, show them some passion.

48 Try and Use the Present Tense

Avoid "I was walking and I saw." It should be "I'm walking and I see." Even if the event happened many, many years ago, you want the audience to be living that moment with you as if it's happening right now. Create the scene for the audience as if it's unfolding in front of their very eyes.

49 Use Inherently Funny Words

Believe it or not, some words are funnier than others and can be amusing without any given context. Quoting Neil Simon, "Words with a 'K' in it are funny. Alka-Seltzer is funny. Chicken is funny. Pickle is funny. All with a 'K.' L's are not funny. M's are not funny." *Simpsons* creator Matt Groening proclaimed the word *underpants* to be at least 15 percent funnier than the word *underwear*. Pants are funny.

"The end of laughter is followed by the height of listening."
—Jeffrey Gitomer

50 Work in References to the Local Area Where Possible

By simply referencing certain affluent areas, calling upon local sporting rivalries, or recognizing challenges or issues pertaining to specific parts of town, you demonstrate that you have a special understanding of and interest in your audience's location.

51 Screen Your Jokes

"Presentations have an extra advantage over most traditional stand-up sets—a giant friggin' screen that the audience is staring at the whole time you're onstage," says Speechless Live creator Sammy Wegent. "In a world where funny Photoshopped images, memes, and GIFs dominate our devices, visual humor has never been bigger. So don't just say funny things in your presentation. Show funny things, too."

52 Make the Image/Video the Proven Punchline

Search sites like Reddit, Imgur, and Pinterest are a great source of funny content that is already socially proven. The key is tying this image to your topic and using it to reinforce a point. Use the same joke structure with images and videos as you would with regular jokes: Set up your image with an introduction that builds anticipation. The image becomes the punch line and should be enough to solicit a laugh, and then you have a chance to keep people laughing through taglines, your additional comments on the image or video.

53 Don't Speak for Too Long

Comedians know their strongest material and know that the best nights are the ones when they do just that. If you are not confident in your ability to speak for forty minutes, ask for less. How about I speak for twenty minutes and allocate twenty additional minutes for Q&A? Conference organizers will seldom rebuff this.

54 Don't Finish on Q&A

Never finish your talk with a questions and answers section. Say, "Now I am going to take a few questions before I make my conclusion." Save a slide for after the Q&A that lists the main points from your talk (ideally three), then deliver your parting words of wisdom.

55 Use Your Hands

"Speak with your hands in front of you, not flopped down to your side," says Matt Morales. "Pretend you're double-fisting a couple of drinks that you're going to spill if you put your arms down. Or just double-fist a couple of beers. Granted, that might not make your presentation better, but eventually you won't care anymore."

56 Make Sure You Are Fully Visible

If there's a podium, try to get out from behind it. If there's a mic stand, once you're comfortable, take the mic out and move the stand to one side. Often the audience needs to see you to fully trust you.

57 Mind Your Face

Your expression is incredibly important from the moment you step on stage to the moment you walk off. Remember to smile. Make eye contact with as many people as you can. Try and build connections.

58 Know Your Audience

This can really help you tailor material and certain jokes to that particular crowd's interest. It can be advantageous if you can get a list of attendees before your conference or presentation and determine where the majority has come from, their average age, job titles, et cetera. If a lot traveled to be there, come from a specific company, or hail from a particular country, it's good to reference this in your presentation and work in some jokes when you can.

59 Be the Host with the Most

If you are acting as the event MC, only reveal the speaker's name with the last words of your introduction. For example, "Ladies and gentlemen, our next speaker is the founder of some wacky startup, an award-winning writer, and occasional low-quality Elvis impersonator. Please give a huge welcome for [their name here]." Saying their name last and only mentioning it at this point builds anticipation and gives the audience their cue to applaud.

"The brain doesn't pay attention to boring things."
–John Medina

60 Add Act-Out

Conversational interaction between two characters gives us the chance to bring the scene to life on stage and put the audience directly into the action. If you can do different voices or different accents or speak another language, work it in. Unless you are really, really good at it, keep it simple. As a guiding principle, *think family members before foreigners!*

61 Do Something Memorable

"This can be good or bad. But memorability is more powerful than likability," says Sammy Obeid.

62 Use Callbacks

Callbacks bring together everything in the end. This is where you go back (call back) and reference items that have had a good reaction or response from the crowd. This can be one of your jokes that worked, or a joke from a previous presenter that got a big laugh.

63 Use Improvisation

Improv often gets the biggest laughs as it appears to occur truly in the moment and creates an in-joke between the speaker and the audience. The most effective comedians combine stand-up, storytelling, and improv techniques. The best business presenters should, too. Don't be afraid to go off script once you have gotten a good, scripted start.

64 Use the Stage

If you have a large stage area to work with, use it to reach people. Connect with them by walking toward them and covering as much of the stage area as you can. Be careful not to nervously sprint around the place. You don't want to distract them or take away from what you're saying.

"Thousands of candles can be lighted from a single candle, and the life of the single candle will not be shortened. Happiness never decreases by being shared."
—Buddha

65 Amp Up Your Punch Line

When you come to the punch line of your joke or the important laugh line, step forward and raise your voice. This combination really emphasizes a point and will further engage the audience. It also gives them their cue to laugh.

66 Don't Forget to Pause

Timing, rhythm, and pauses become really important. A proper pause can help create curiosity within an audience. Give them a chance to catch their breath, build tension, and then, BANG! You burst into the laugh line. Small changes in delivery like raising your voice at the end of a sentence have a big, big impact. Comedians say there is no substitute for stage time to improve timing. While this is true in part, what mainly happens over time is that one masters the delivery of tested stories and laugh lines.

67 Let Them Laugh

Once you get them laughing, shut up, allow them time to laugh and enjoy the moment. Only start to speak again when the laughter starts to dwindle to just a couple of people.

68 Keep All Material and Stories Clean

As a rule of thumb, if what you are talking about is below the waist-line, leave it out.

69 Never Ignore Interruptions

If it's annoying you, it is probably annoying the audience as well. Just make sure it's actually happening before closing off any unwanted intrusion. Always be polite unless you really, really have no other option. Remember, you control the audience.

"A sense of humor is part of the art of leadership, of getting along with people, of getting things done."
–Dwight D. Eisenhower

70 Repeat, Pause, and Play

Often the best way to deal with an intrusion or comment is simply to repeat that comment. If it was an obviously stupid question, by simply repeating it and pausing for effect the audience will likely laugh spontaneously. To add easy laughs, intentionally mispronounce or misinterpret one of their key words.

71 Don't Pet the Hamster

New and experienced speakers alike tend to couple their hands nervously in front of their body almost as if they are petting a hamster. Leave the hamster at home and consciously catch yourself every time you stroke the imaginary little fur ball.

72 Command Attention

Next time the audience is still chatting or not quite settled, stop and ask them to clap if they can hear you. Once a few begin to clap, keep it going until those who were talking shut up and join in. They will. Like birds flocking together, people naturally behave as a group. They will assume you said something interesting worthy of applause, fear they missed something awesome, and join in. Now you reset and start again. It never fails. "Clap if you can hear me."

73 Trust Your Funny Bits

"Your jokes are funny, so have confidence in them," says Brandon Scott Wolf. "Deliver your punch lines emphatically, and then give the audience a moment or two to process what you said so they can laugh."

74 Keep Boring to Yourself

"Don't put something out there that bores you. If it bores you to tell it, you can bet it will bore your audience to hear it," says Sal Calanni.

"Nothing will work unless you do."
—Maya Angelou

75 Proper Planning Prevents Poor Performance

Over-preparation will help you be ready for anything. The knowledge and confidence that you can handle whatever comes your way on stage will assuage some of the fear you might be feeling. With calm nerves, rehearsed delivery, and material you know through and through, you will look better on stage than you could ever hope to without consistent practice. After all, as Steve Martin says, "Persistence is a great substitute for talent."

76 Never Run the Clock

Practice your timing and aim to never, ever go over the allocated time limit. If there isn't a set time limit to go by, make sure that you impose one on yourself. This forces you to go back and strip out unnecessary words or information and be a minimalist. Use the fewest words with the greatest impact.

77 Know Your Section Times

Break down each talk into components, record them, and know how long it takes to tell each (e.g., intro, pitch, additional details, numbers component, lessons, and main takeaways). Knowing the associated times for each part will help you craft the perfect performance and facilitate quickly making changes if your time slot is cut.

78 Stay in Permanent Beta

Video- or audio-record every time you're on stage and review it. Be pleased but never satisfied with every performance. The idea of being in Permanent Beta, that there's always room for improvement, is a perspective that will set you up for success.

79 Enjoy Yourself

Have fun, play, and be creative. If you're having fun, others will, too.

"The whole object of comedy is to be yourself. The closer to that you get, the funnier you will be."
—Jerry Seinfeld

And last but not least, from Irish comedian Dylan Moran:

80 Don't Rely on Potential

"Don't do it! Stay away from your potential," Moran says. "You'll mess it up. It's potential; leave it. Anyway, it's like your bank balance—you always have a lot less than you think."

As Mark Twain said, "The human race has only one really effective weapon and that is laughter." That type of arms race may be one worth all our time. Most presentations are really boring. By applying these tips, yours will not be.

These eighty tips can be obtained free at http://www.7comedy-habits.com/80tips. If you know anyone who could really use them, please do share!

Acknowledgments

Overcoming this fear and all the fun had along the way could not have been possible without the following fine folks:

My parents, Patrick and Marita Nihill, who always support me no matter how wacky my plans may be. My initial editor, Nils Parker, who brought the funny and legibility when I could not; and Debbie Harmsen, whose fine skills I had the privilege of having on my side with this updated version. To Andrea Somberg, Glenn Yeffeth, and the great folks at BenBella for their wisdom, hard work, and support in getting this book in front of you. Ana Carolina Fujihara, for never telling me this experiment was a bad idea, among many, many other wonderful things. Arash Bayatmakou, for continually inspiring through his amazing achievements and his constant feedback throughout. Inanc Karacaylak and Josh Cereghino, for helping open many doors that often do their best to stay firmly closed.

So many others have lent their wisdom and support along the way: Philip Madden, David Howley, Matt Ellsworth, Max Altschuler, Jordan Harbinger, Mauricio Vergara, Rachman Blake, Debbie Dowling, Tim Lee, William McCarthy, Darragh Moher, Aram Fischer, Tom Morkes, Laura Bekes, Erin Tyler, Peter McGraw, Alex McClafferty, David Ryan, Eve Grenon-LaFontaine, Darragh Flynn, Sal Calanni, Ronan Collins, Kabir

Singh, Matt Morales, Guy Vincent, Emily Epstein White, Maria Gagliano, Bill Grundfest, James Ward, Angelica H. Salceda, Jeff Zamaria, Michael Margolis, Chris Lindland, Richard Sarvate, Andrew Stanley, Jeff Kreisler, Hugh Gurin, Laura Montini, Andrew Tarvin, Scott Sanders, Doug Cordell, Tiffany Richeson, Don Reed, Brittany Kamerschen, Mark McMillian, James Dilworth, Jason Steinberg, David Spinks, Gil Zeimer, Andrew Slusser, Anna Mackinnon, Bob Ayres, and many more.

Stage time, stage time, stage time: A huge thanks to all those who gave me the time to stand on theirs. Doors that were hard to open kept on opening due to you.

A massive thanks to all the hilarious comedians who gave their time and talents to be part of Comedy for a Spinal Cause: Tim Lee, Scott Capurro, Kellin Erskine, Sal Calanni, Reggie Steele, Matt Morales, Kabir Singh, Brendan Lynch, Daymon Ferguson, Drennon Davis, Nick Stargu, Josef Anolin, Joe Tobin, Kevin Munroe, Cody Woods, Ben Feldman, Red Scott, Iris Benson, Kaseem Bentley, Sandra Risser, Clay Newman, Dan St. Paul, Arthur Gaus, Chad Opitz, Juan Medina, Emily Van Dyke, Jonny Ellar, Kate Willett, Matt Lieb, Stroy Moyd, Dhaya Lakshminarayanan, and Matt Gubser. Laughter never did so much good.

There is no reason these nights cannot be run in every major city. Comedians need new audiences and stage time; people with spinal cord injuries need the funds for much-needed therapy. We all need laughter. If you can help make this a reality please get in touch.

If you need help adding the funny, drop us a line via help@
funnybizz.co. Through my company, FunnyBizz (http://funny-
bizz.co), you can access a team of top comedic talent that spe-
cializes in making all forms of written content funnier.

Notes

Introduction

1. Taken from Carmine Gallo's talks and his article, "9 Public-Speaking Lessons From The World's Greatest TED Talks," *Forbes,* March 4, 2014, http://www. forbes.com/sites/carminegallo/2014/03/04/9-public -speaking-lessons-from-the-worlds-greatest-ted-talks/.
2. Tim Ferriss, "Public Speaking—How I Prepare Every Time," *The Tim Ferriss Experiment* (blog), April 11, 2010, http://fourhourworkweek.com/2010/04/11 /public-speaking-how-i-prepare-every-time/.

Chapter 1

3. Jason Miller, "Meet the Marketer: Ann Handley & Her Magical Mix of Content Marketing Tips," *LinkedIn Marketing Solutions Blog,* September 15, 2014, http://marketing.linkedin.com/blog/meet-the -marketer-ann-handley-her-magical-mix-of-content -marketing-tips/.

4. Harrison Monarth, "The Irresistible Power of Storytelling as a Strategic Business Tool," *Harvard Business Review*, March 11, 2014, https://hbr.org /2014/03/the-irresistible-power-of-storytelling-as-a -strategic-business-tool.

5. Gary Vaynerchuk, "Stop Storytelling Like It's 2007," YouTube video, 16:07, posted by "99U," February 6, 2014, https://www.youtube.com /watch?v=OnXijAxiy8g.

6. Heidi Cohen, "Seth Godin: 7 Truths at the Heart of Marketing (& How to Use Them)," December 14, 2011, http://heidicohen.com/seth-godin-7-truths-at -the-heart-of-marketing-how-to-use-them/.

7. Dave Kerpen, "5 Keys to Great Storytelling: Lessons from Barbara Corcoran," *WordofMouth.org*, December 12, 2013, http://wordofmouth.org/blog/5 -keys-to-great-storytelling-lessons-from-barbara -corcoran/.

8. Steven Pressfield, "The Inciting Incident," *Steven Pressfield Online,* February 2, 2011, http://www .stevenpressfield.com/2011/02/the-inciting-incident/.

9. BrainyQuote, "Steven Spielberg Quotes," n.d., http:// www.brainyquote.com/quotes/quotes/s /stevenspie398353.html; Wikiquote, "Steven Spielberg," n.d., https://en.wikiquote.org/wiki /Steven_Spielberg.

10. Richard Fitzpatrick, "C'mere Till I Tell Ya: The Art of Storytelling," *The Irish Times,* August 23, 2014, http:// www.irishtimes.com/culture/c-mere-till-i-tell-ya-the- art-of-storytelling-1.1901635.

11. Mike Birbiglia, "Act One: Error at First Base," *This American Life,* Episode 411: "First Contact," June 25,

2010, http://www.thisamericanlife.org/radio-archives
/episode/411/first-contact?act=1.

12. The Moth, "Storytelling Tips," n.d., http://themoth
.org/tell-a-story/storytelling-tips.

Chapter 2

13. Samuel Bacharach, "Leadership without Presumption:
Lessons from Eisenhower," *Inc.,* June 26, 2013, http://
www.inc.com/samuel-bacharach/leadership-without
-presumption-lessons-from-eisenhower.html.

14. Martha Craumer, "Getting Serious about Workplace
Humor," *Harvard Communication Letter,* July 2002.

15. R. Cronin, *Humor in the Workplace* (Rosemont, IL:
Hodge-Cronin and Associates, 1997).

16. All are referenced in Andrew J. Tarvin, *Humor That
Works: Why You Should Use Humor and How to Get
Started,* http://www.humorthatworks.com
/files/HumorThatWorks_Book.pdf; Steve Bannister,
"Making Sense of Humour in the Workplace,"
CanadaOne, September 30, 2006, http://www
.canadaone.com/ezine/oct06/humour_at_work.html.

17. *Business Interviews*, interview with Andrew Tarvin,
June 4, 2013, http://www.businessinterviews.com
/humor-that-works-andrew-tarvin.

18. "Reagan-Mondale Debate: The Age Issue," YouTube
video, 0:40, posted by "lawford83," June 25, 2008,
https://www.youtube.com/watch?v=LoPu1UIBkBc.

19. Steve Allen, "Steve Allen's Almanac," *Cosmopolitan*,
February 1957, 12.

20. Susan Tardanico, "Who Says You're Not Funny?
Tips from Top Humorist Jeanne Robertson," *Forbes,*
August 14, 2012, http://www.forbes.com/sites

/susantardanico/2012/08/14/who-says-youre-not
-funny-tips-from-top-humorist-jeanne-robertson/.

21. John Kinde, "The Rule of Three: A Humor Technique
from the World of Comedy," *John Kinde's Humor
Power,* 2006, http://www.humorpower.com/art
-rulethree.html.

22. "CNN: SOTU Address, President Obama Cracks
Smoked Salmon Joke," YouTube video, 0:44, posted
by "CNN," January 25, 2011, https://www.youtube
.com/watch?v=BFcWz9eyovA.

Chapter 3

23. "John F. Kennedy Rice University Moon Speech,"
YouTube video, 2:02, posted by "Spaceflight,"
June 20, 2009, https://www.youtube.com
/watch?v=_RaRC6YuYCQ.

24. Taken from Groening's DVD commentaries; Ann
Althouse, "When One Word Is Funnier Than
Another," *Althouse* (blog), February 3, 2007, http://
althouse.blogspot.ie/2007/02/when-one-word-is
-funnier-than-another.html.

25. Scott Adams, "Writing Funny," *Dilbert Blog*, July 13,
2007, http://dilbertblog.typepad.com/the_dilbert
_blog/2007/07/writing-funny.html.

Chapter 4

26. Steve Martin, *Born Standing Up* (New York:
Scribner, 2008).

27. Vanessa Van Edwards, "5 Secrets of a Successful
TED Talk," *Science of People,* n.d., http://www.
scienceofpeople.com/5-secrets-of-a-successful

-ted-talk-2/; Alison Prato, "Does Body Language Help a TED Talk Go Viral? 5 Nonverbal Patterns from Blockbuster Talks," *TEDBlog,* May 12, 2015, http://blog.ted.com/body-language-survey-points-to-5-nonverbal-features-that-make-ted-talks-take-off.

28. Annette Ferrara, "Your Presentation Needs a Punch Line," *Harvard Business Review,* May 21, 2015, https://hbr.org/2015/05/your-presentation-needs-a-punch-line.

29. "Big Question: Why Do You Hate the Sound of Your Own Voice?" *Marquette Magazine,* Summer 2014, http://www.marquette.edu/magazine/recent.php?subaction=showfull&id=1260897469/.

30. Jordan Gaines, "Why You Hate the Sound of Your Own Voice," *NBC News,* April 2, 2013, http://bodyodd.nbcnews.com/_news/2013/04/02/17557410-why-you-hate-the-sound-of-your-own-voice.

31. Joshua Foer, "Feats of Memory Anyone Can Do," TED video, 20:28, February 2012, http://www.ted.com/talks/joshua_foer_feats_of_memory_anyone_can_do?language=en.

32. Martin, *Born Standing Up.*

33. Lucy Kellaway, "Why It Is Very Clever to Pretend to Be Stupid," *Financial Times,* November 10, 2013, http://www.ft.com/cms/s/0/fdbc8282-4859-11e3-a3ef-00144feabdc0.html#axzz3nj1ujckl.

34. Mikael Cho, "Want to Be a Better Storyteller? Learn from a Comedian," *Crew* (blog), n.d., https://blog.crew.co/want-to-be-a-better-storyteller-learn-from-a-comedian/; Soon Min Yap, "How Stand-Up Comedians Handle the Challenges of Pitching," *LinkedIn Pulse* (blog), October 12, 2014, https://www.linkedin.com/pulse/20141012161005-178582097

-how-stand-up-comedians-handle-the-challenges-of-pitching.

35. Juliet Barbara, "Twitter CEO Dick Costolo Urges Graduates to 'Be in the Moment,'" *Forbes,* May 5, 2013, http://www.forbes.com/sites/julietbarbara/2013/05/05/twitter-ceo-dick-costolo-urges-graduates-to-be-in-this-moment/.

36. Jonah Weiner, "Jerry Seinfeld Intends to Die Standing Up," *New York Times Magazine,* December 20, 2012, http://www.nytimes.com/2012/12/23/magazine/jerry-seinfeld-intends-to-die-standing-up.html?_r=0.

37. Barry M. Kudrowitz, "Haha and Aha! Creativity, Idea Generation, Improvisational Humor, and Product Design," DSpace@MIT, 2010, http://dspace.mit.edu/handle/1721.1/61610.

Chapter 7

38. Arash Bayatmakou, "SCI Survey: Results and Summary," *Arash Recovery* (blog), March 11, 2014, http://arashrecovery.com/2014/03/11/sci-survey-results-and-summary.

39. Jerry Weissman, "How to Remember What to Say and Four Ways to Make It Stick," *Forbes,* April 20, 2015, http://www.forbes.com/sites/jerryweissman/2015/04/20/how-to-remember-what-to-say-and-four-ways-to-make-it-stick.

40. Andrew Bender, "Top 10 Funniest Movies Ever (As Measured in Laughs per Minute)," *Forbes,* September 21, 2012, http://www.forbes.com/sites/andrewbender/2012/09/21/top-10-funniest-movies-ever-as-measured-in-laughs-per-minute.

Conclusion

41. James Altucher, *Choose Yourself* (Amazon Digital Services, 2013); summary here: Davin Paul, "80/20 Review of 'Choose Yourself' by James Altucher," *Davin Paul* (blog), August 3, 2013, http://davinpaul .com/8020-review-of-choose-yourself-by-james -altucher-2/.

42. Altucher, *Choose Yourself.*

43. Comedy for a Spinal Cause (Facebook community), https://www.facebook.com/comedyforaspinalcause.

About the Author

David was born in Dublin, Ireland. After graduating with a master's degree in business in 2003, he moved to San Francisco, where he worked for the Irish government helping startups expand rapidly. He has been involved with startup companies ever since. David is the founder of FunnyBizz, a community, conference series, and writer platform helping content creators tap into the power of storytelling, comedy, and improv to create better content. He has performed stand-up comedy at California's leading clubs including Cobb's, the Comedy Store, the Improv, and the Punchline even though he strongly denies being a comedian and is well aware most people don't understand his accent. His learning, taken from one year's intensive experiments in comedy, performed on someone from the business community with a huge initial fear of public speaking (i.e., him!), has been featured in *Inc.*, Lifehacker, and *Forbes*, among others. He loves sharks, still dislikes public speaking, and calls San Francisco home when immigration officials permit.